Biological Perspectives in Developmental Psychology

Life-Span Human Development Series
Series Editors: Freda Rebelsky, Boston University, and Lynn Dorman

Infancy
Kathryn Sherrod, George Peabody College for Teachers
Peter Vietze, George Peabody College for Teachers
Steven Friedman, South Shore Mental Health Center

Early Childhood
Donald L. Peters, The Pennsylvania State University
Sherry L. Willis, The Pennsylvania State University

The Middle Years of Childhood
Patricia Minuchin, Temple University

Adolescence
Kathleen M. White, Boston University
Joseph C. Speisman, Boston University

Early and Middle Adulthood
Lillian E. Troll, Rutgers University

Late Adulthood: Perspectives on Human Development
Richard A. Kalish, Berkeley, California

Cross-Cultural Human Development
Robert L. Munroe, Pitzer College
Ruth H. Munroe, Pitzer College

Life-Span Developmental Psychology:
Introduction to Research Methods
Paul B. Baltes, The Pennsylvania State University
Hayne W. Reese, West Virginia University
John R. Nesselroade, The Pennsylvania State University

Biological Perspectives in Developmental Psychology
George F. Michel, University of Massachusetts
Celia L. Moore, University of Massachusetts

Biological Perspectives in Developmental Psychology

George F. Michel

University of Massachusetts

Celia L. Moore

University of Massachusetts

BROOKS/COLE PUBLISHING COMPANY
MONTEREY, CALIFORNIA
A Division of Wadsworth Publishing Company, Inc. 0347574

Printed in the United States of America

10 9 8 7 6 5 4 3 2 1

Library of Congress Cataloging in Publication Data

Michel, George F., 1944–
    Biological perspectives in developmental psychology.

    (Brooks/Cole life-span human development series)
    Bibliography: p. 110
    Includes indexes.
    1. Developmental psychology.   2. Psychology.
I. Moore, Celia L., 1942–   joint author.
II. Title.
BF713.M53   155   77-26003
ISBN 0-8185-0260-6

Acquisition Editor: *Todd Lueders*
Production Editor: *Valerie Faraday Daigen*
Interior and Cover Design: *Linda Marcetti*
Cover Illustration: *Jim Pinckney*
Typesetting: *Boyer & Brass, Inc., San Diego, California*

Series Foreword

What are the changes we see over the life span? How can we explain them? And how do we account for individual differences? The Life-Span Human Development Series provides a new way to look at these questions. It approaches human development from three major perspectives: (1) a focus on basic issues related to the study of life-span developmental psychology, such as methodology and research design, cross-cultural and longitudinal studies, age-stage phenomena, and stability and change; (2) a focus on age divisions—infancy, early childhood, middle childhood, adolescence, young and middle adulthood, and late adulthood; and (3) a focus on developmental areas such as physiology, cognition, language, perception, sex roles, and personality.

There is some overlap in the content of these volumes. We believe that it will be stimulating to the reader to think the same idea through from the viewpoints of different authors or from the viewpoints of different areas of development. For example, language development is the subject of one volume and is also discussed in the volume on cross-cultural development, among others.

Instructors and students may use the entire series for a thorough survey of life-span developmental psychology or, since each volume can be used independently, may choose selected volumes to cover specific concept areas or age ranges. Volumes that focus on basic issues can be used to introduce the student to the life-span concept.

No single author could adequately cover the entire field as we have defined it. Our authors found it exciting to focus on their areas of specialization within a limited space while, at the same time, expanding their thinking to encompass the entire life span. It can be beneficial to both author and student to attempt a new integration of familiar material. Since we think it also benefits students to see ideas in development, we encouraged the authors not only to review the relevant literature but also to use what they now know to point up possible new areas of study. As a result, the student will learn to think about human development rather than just learn the facts of development.

Freda Rebelsky

Lynn Dorman

For D. S. L.

Preface

The field of developmental psychology appears to be moving toward a state of maturity or, at least, toward another change in stage. This transition is marked by an increasing dissatisfaction on the part of developmental psychologists with many of the approaches that have become staples of the discipline over the past several years. Gone is the enthusiasm of previous decades for charting milestones of psychological development over age. Similarly, examination of the course of development in relation to such common demographic characteristics of human populations as socioeconomic class, ethnic-group membership, race, culture, and sex has lost much of its appeal. These standard approaches have proven far more limited than was anticipated in their ability to shed light on the causes of development, and so there has arisen a deliberate, if unsystematic, search for a new framework.

It is not surprising that searches for new approaches to developmental psychology have often focused on the biological disciplines. This is in part attributable to the fact that biology has become a fashionable discipline during the past two decades. There is a growing belief that new biological techniques and concepts will profoundly influence the course of human societies, much as physics and chemistry have done over the past 200 years. There is also growing reason to believe that biological concepts and ideas will have much to contribute to developmental psychology. Indeed, the next two decades may be witness to a successful merging of biology with developmental psychology.

In this book, we provide the reader with some basic information about various biological disciplines so that a beginning may be made toward an understanding of these trends. We also provide a conceptual framework that we believe will help the reader appreciate the interrelationship of developmental psychology and biology. The framework we provide will not ultimately be the best, nor is it currently the most popular. However, we feel that it is the most fruitful and most acceptable framework that is currently available. It is the most fruitful because it emphasizes the bidirectional nature of the relationship between biology and developmental psychology, thereby preserving an active, constructive role for the developmental psychologist and allowing for the inclusion of much of the current research in cognitive, social, and behavioral development of humans within a biologically oriented framework. It is the most acceptable because it is supported by a growing body of empirical evidence that does not fit the more widely known alternative frameworks. Because our conceptual framework encompasses perspectives from both biology and developmental psychology, we have decided to call it a developmental-psychobiological approach.

As one of the volumes in the Brooks/Cole Life-Span Human Development Series, this book can be used to supplement a basic text in developmental psychology or to complement a number of basic or supplementary texts on any stage of the human life span. It is also appropriate for use as a core text in undergraduate courses in developmental psychobiology or ethological psychology in departments of psychology, biology, anthropology, or human development.

Of course, in such a small book it is not possible to introduce the student to all of the aspects of modern biology, psychology, and psychobiology that are relevant to issues of development. It is also impossible to integrate comprehensively into our approach the major areas of research on human development. We have chosen instead to present as clearly as possible a developmental-psychobiological approach that can be used as a guide by readers who wish to venture into these interdisciplinary regions. Throughout the book we point to instances in which research in human developmental psychology can be viewed from biological perspectives. The reader should feel encouraged to find other instances. We also try to present the case that humans and their behavior will be better understood, and better appreciated, when the membership of human beings in the animal kingdom is recognized. It is our hope that this book, and others like it, will serve to alter the format of undergraduate courses in developmental psychology toward a less anthropocentric and more holistic presentation of developmental issues and research.

Writing a book is often a frustrating and prolonged experience involving many set and missed deadlines. We would like to thank our series editors, Freda Rebelsky and Lynn Dorman, and our Brooks/Cole editor, Todd Lueders, for their patience and encouragement. We especially thank our production editor, Valerie Daigen, for diligently correcting our grammatical errors and increasing the clarity of our presentation. Both Robert B. Cairns of the University of North Carolina and Richard M. Lerner of the Pennsylvania State University reviewed an earlier draft of the manuscript and provided encouragement and advice beyond what one would expect of friends, much less strangers. We would like to thank them and note that any conceptual or empirical limitations in the present work stem entirely from us. We would also like to thank Carolyn J. Mebert, who not only did all of the illustrations but also provided detailed comments on much of the material in this book as an undergraduate and again as a graduate student. Finally, we owe a debt, beyond our ability to repay, to Daniel Lehrman, whose ideas, enthusiasm, knowledge, insight into conceptual issues, and humane and sensitive approach to the social aspects of science have served as a model for our development as scientists.

George F. Michel
Celia L. Moore

Contents

Biological
Perspectives
in Developmental
Psychology

Chapter One

Biology in the Origins of Developmental and Comparative Psychology

It is likely that on many occasions you have sat in a public park and watched a squirrel leap from branch to branch, run down to the ground, dig about at the base of a tree trunk, retrieve an acorn, and eat it. This is a rather common event in the daily life of a familiar organism. You may have merely noted it as a fact of life, you may have remarked on the skill and grace of the squirrel, or you may have become curious about the event.

If you consider for a moment all the things one might want to know about the event of a squirrel eating an acorn, you may find that you have, in effect, enumerated all of the subdivisions or disciplines within biology. Biologists are persons who elaborate curiosity about living organisms into a profession; *biology* is often defined simply as the study of life.

Taking a biological perspective, you might ask what effect the squirrel's activities have on oak trees or on other animals that eat acorns. What effect does the availability of oak trees have on the distribution of squirrels in the area? What is it about the squirrel's physiology that leads it to eat the acorn at one time rather than at another? Is there anything unique about the anatomy or physiology of the squirrel that makes eating acorns more appropriate than eating insects or birds? How is the available acorn supply divided among the different squirrels that live in the neighborhood? Are there other animals that get food in a manner similar to the squirrel's, and, if so, why are there these similarities? What animals are evolutionarily related to squirrels? Are the food-getting activities of these animals similar to or different from the food-getting activities of squirrels, and why?

"But," you may argue, "why raise all of these biological questions? The event you have described is a behavioral event, and it raises many questions about perception, perceptual-motor coordination, learning, motivation, and behavioral development. Such questions are psychological questions."

Now suppose that both psychologists and biologists become interested in explaining the same phenomenon. An observer might ask what

1

differences, if any, exist in their descriptions and explanations of the phenomenon and how these differences can be synthesized into a single account of the phenomenon. These are the questions that we intend to address, particularly as they have been raised within the discipline of developmental psychology.

The role of the biological disciplines in developmental psychology is neither obvious nor straightforward. Although interdisciplinary relationships are necessarily complex, there are many misconceptions commonly held about the content and concerns of both disciplines that unnecessarily add to the complexity. Biology is usually thought to be the study of animals, plants, and the functioning of body tissues and organs, whereas psychology is thought to be concerned with mind, emotions, motives, personality, and social relations and the development of all of these. Although these notions are partially correct, they create an artificial division that leaves both fields incompletely defined, and this incompleteness in turn gives a highly ambiguous status to certain subject matter. What does one do with areas, such as human neuropsychology or animal behavior, that cannot be placed in one field or the other?

If one defines biology as the study of life, then, because the subject matter of psychology is clearly an aspect of the study of life, it follows that the various psychological disciplines ought to be considered subdivisions of biology. However, it is often more useful to define scientific disciplines by the questions they ask rather than by the phenomena they examine. As we will show later, it is not important whether behavior is studied as biology or as psychology. What is important is the type of question asked about the behavior and how the answers to different questions may be interrelated.

By asking what unifies the traditional biological disciplines into a common science, one may arrive at a historical reason for the fact that psychology is not frequently thought of as a part of biology. Although biological disciplines are quite diverse and frequently appear to be far apart on many issues, they are unified in at least three ways. The first way is by their common subject matter: life. Second, they are unified by their shared acceptance of the modern theory of evolution. The third way is best characterized by the notion of tradition. Traditions in science arise from common features and historical continuity in the character of professional training. Since the late 19th century, there has been a growing divergence in the professional training of biologists and psychologists that has led to separate traditions. As the two disciplines gained members, widened their subject matter, and developed new techniques of investigation, their students began to focus on separate sets of course materials and to feel connected with different historical antecedents. Psychologists began to trace their interests back to philosophical concerns about how people acquire and use knowledge—how they come to know, regulate, and cope with their existence. In contrast, biologists came to trace their interests to philosophical concerns with the order of living creatures and the functioning of their parts. As a result of these differences, successive generations of students in both psychology and biology began to be exposed to separate sets of course materials and techniques of investigation during their training. Because the number of theories, phenomena, and techniques in the province of each discipline has mushroomed during the past 50 years, it has become very difficult for students of one discipline to obtain more than a smattering of exposure to the content and conceptual frameworks of the other. Therefore, students of each discipline can view the other discipline only from a perspective of ignorance and popular bias.

Thus, today, when biologists and psychologists come to share an interest in some subject, they are less likely to be as familiar with each other's theories, concepts, and methods than are scientists from the various subdivisions within either biology or psychology. This lack of familiarity with each other's traditions, because it allows the examination of phenomena from fresh perspectives, can have the positive effect of stimulating further development. Unfortunately, the lack of familiarity often results in some animosity, a good deal of confusion, and the creation of pseudoproblems. A pseudoproblem is one that has no means of solution or that can be solved only through clarification of concepts or of the way in which the question is stated and not through further examination of the phenomenon in question.

We contend that the integration of biological disciplines and psychology can be mutually beneficial. The richness of biology can only increase with the incorporation of psychology, and the concepts, theories, and techniques of psychology require the perspective of biology for their refinement. Moreover, such an integration can lead to the identification of significant new phenomena and problems, the clarification of explanatory concepts, and the solution to old, seemingly insoluble problems and pseudoproblems plaguing both disciplines. In terms of the field of behavioral development, the integration of biology and psychology can lead to the discovery that development is influenced by factors hitherto regarded either as unlikely to be related to development or as theoretically uninteresting. Fortunately, current trends seem to mark an increasing interest in the removal of the boundaries separating disciplines and the introduction of interdisciplinary examinations of behavioral phenomena; witness the construction of a field alternately referred to as *psychobiology* and *biopsychology*. This book, as an introduction to developmental psychobiology, is also an attempt to clear away the cobwebs from people's thinking about humans as animals.

The Hazards of the Interdisciplinary Endeavor

In the past several years it has become quite fashionable for psychologists and psychiatrists in the field of child development to direct their attention to the role of "biology" in psychological development. The focus of this attention has often come to rest on those scientists involved in the study of animal behavior, particularly in the field of ethology. The ethologist is concerned with understanding the behavior of animals as completely as possible. Developing this understanding means not only systematically describing an animal's behavior and identifying the social and environmental situations affecting the occurrence of this behavior but also describing the evolutionary and developmental history of the behavior and exploring the physiological mechanisms involved in its organization. Given this broad domain of concern, ethology appears to be an area in which biology and psychology can be integrated.

With such attention directed toward their work, ethologists are often faced with the question "What is it that students of child development would like to know about or would find helpful in animal-behavior studies?" As Lehrman (1974) points out, this question suggests the most pernicious problem facing any cross-disciplinary exchange of information—the distortion of meaning. To understand this problem, you must recognize that scientific disciplines are distinguishable not only by their content but also by the way in which nature is viewed. In other words, there is a context of methods, techniques, interests, and aims uniquely associated with a particular scientific discipline that contributes to the meaning of the concepts and terms it uses and to the meaning of the phenomena and data it derives. This means that extracting some phenomenon or concept from the context of its discipline for the purpose of using it in another discipline robs it of some of the essential components of its meaning. People frequently experience this distortion in meaning when they try to relate an amusing incident in their life to a casual acquaintance. Lacking the enrichment provided by knowledge of the other and of the circumstances of the situation, the listener never fully appreciates the humor of the incident. So, too, may the biologist or psychologist not fully appreciate the meanings of concepts and phenomena drawn from the other discipline.

Consider, for example, the concept of imprinting. As originally used in ethological studies, this concept *described* specific behaviors in the young of certain bird species. These behaviors included primarily the establishment, as a result of early exposure to the parent, of following of the parent soon after hatching, preference for the parent as a social companion, and selection of a mate from the parent's species when the young bird became sexually mature. The identification of these behaviors as the occurrence of imprinting was achieved by a specific set of experimental operations. First, the young bird had to be shown to have no preference for any particular thing as an object of its social responses unless it had been exposed to some stimulus—a moving box or flashing light, for example—for a certain period of time shortly after hatching. After exposing the animal to the stimulus, the researcher assessed the young bird's social preference by comparing its behavior toward the previously experienced stimulus with its behavior toward an unfamiliar stimulus. If the bird preferred to follow or stay in the vicinity of the stimulus to which it was previously exposed rather than to respond in these ways to the new stimulus, imprinting could be said to have occurred. Contrary to early opinion, the choice of an object of adult sexual behavior has been found to be a relatively unreliable criterion for imprinting. That is to say, the class of object (for example, species) from which a mate is selected need not be the same as that to which filial social responses were preferentially directed. Not only has the notion that imprinting permanently and exclusively determines a duck's or goose's preferences for social and sexual partners been questioned by recent research, but researchers have also shown that imprinting does not involve a unique learning process. As a result, the concept of imprinting has been extended to include any preference resulting from early exposure to some stimulus and has been used to describe habitat, food, and companion preferences in a variety of animals, including some mammalian species.

Recently, the concept of imprinting has been extracted from the field of ethology and applied to human development. In its new context, the concept has been used to *explain,* among other things, the formation and maintenance of mother–infant emotional and social relations (for example, Bowlby, 1969), early infantile autism (for example, Moore & Shiek, 1971), adult infant-carrying positions (Salk, 1973), the soothing effects of certain sounds (Salk, 1962), and adult psychosexual fetishes (Sutherland, 1963).

Thus, although most ethologists have been careful to use the imprinting concept as a descriptive label for a class of phenomena having certain characteristics, imprinting has frequently been used as an explanatory concept, particularly in the human literature. This practice is unfortunate. First, although it has been argued that the human infant undergoes an imprinting process that is the same as that observed in birds, it is rarely the case that the operations defining imprinting in birds have been applied to humans. The stimuli to which the infant is exposed are seldom manipulated, and preferences are often inadequately assessed. Further, the imprinting concept serves as merely a nominal explanation for some observed preference. In the statement "Human infants prefer their own mothers because they have been imprinted to them," the word *because* is meaningless; *imprinting* is simply a term that restates the observed preference. By accepting a word as the explanation (that is, by accepting a nominal explanation), the scientist becomes less likely to search for the factors responsible for the formation of social preferences.

Because imprinting was originally associated with the concepts of *critical period* and *irreversibility* in ethology, these subsidiary notions have often been assimilated into human studies. Yet there has been little recognition, in the human studies, of the changes in use and meaning of these terms within ethology. The concept of critical period, for example, has been replaced by that of *sensitive period* by ethologists because research has shown that the time period during which exposure to a stimulus will lead to imprinting can be altered by appropriate environmental changes (Moltz & Stettner, 1961). That is, whereas it is possible to determine the time period during which exposure to certain stimuli is most likely to result in imprinting, it is possible for imprinting to occur during other time periods, provided that the stimuli are appropriate and the exposure long enough (for example, Bateson, 1966, 1973). Imprinting can occur even outside the time boundaries of the sensitive period, and recent evidence indicates that it can occur with multiple stimuli as effectively as with a single stimulus. It is these essential changes in the meaning of the imprinting concept that have been lost in the extraction of the concept from the animal literature and the injection of it into the study of human development.

The imprinting example also illustrates a further problem in cross-disciplinary transfer of concepts. That is, concepts developed in the pursuit of the answer to a question intrinsic to one discipline frequently become attached to a question intrinsic to a second discipline, merely because of some resemblance between the two questions (for example, "Why does the duckling prefer its parent?" and "Why does the infant prefer its parent?"). As the concept moves from its original context to a new one, it is necessarily adjusted (distorted) to fit. For example, imprinting, redefined as attachment, has been assimilated into psychoanalytic conceptions of object relations and entangled with conceptions of dependency. Distortion of this nature is an unavoidable consequence of cross-disciplinary endeavors. It should not be taken lightly, however, nor should the problem of changed meaning of transplanted facts and concepts be left unstated. To avoid this issue is to be both misleading and confusing—to act in a way that is contrary to the fundamental tenets of science.

Of course, investigators' best protection against being misled by cross-disciplinary distortion of meaning involves becoming as familiar with allied disciplines as they are with their own. Obviously, it is not often possible for investigators to develop this familiarity, and so this solution is, at the least, impractical. However, researchers can gain some protection from the conceptual problems inherent in cross-disciplinary work by reading widely in the literature of those disciplines bordering on their own, thereby increasing the range of phenomena and concepts not directly related to their own interests that they can appreciate. In this way, investigators can increase their sensitivity to the context in which borrowed concepts that are relevant to their own discipline derive their meaning. Another means of protection from distortion is the adoption of an attitude or a conceptual framework flexible enough to incorporate, unchanged, concepts from many disciplines.

It is our intention in this book to give you, the psychology student, some background in the biological disciplines, so that you can meet in context the biological concepts and phenomena that are relevant to the study of child development. In addition, we wish to acquaint you with a conceptual framework for the study of developmental psychobiology that we believe removes much of the confusion and deception that can otherwise accompany interdisciplinary study. To do these things requires that we turn your attention to the histories of these disciplines.

The Darwinian Legacy

Evidence of biology's influence can be found throughout the recorded history of developmental psychology. In fact, the publication of Darwin's theory of evolution played a key role in the formation of developmental psychology as a discipline. Darwin's theory was also highly instrumental in the formation of a sister discipline—comparative psychology. Comparative and developmental psychology continued to have much in common, and we contend that they still have much to contribute to each other. We believe that both fields *require us to think carefully about organisms that differ from us in important ways and to think about the relationships connecting these different organisms to us.*

Both of these psychological disciplines have borrowed much from biology. The most important loan from biology was the recognition of the continuity between human beings and other animals. This recognition not only brought about a shift in perspective regarding the traditional subject matter of psychology—the adult human—but also shifted psychology's realm of interest to include children and other animals. If the human being is an animal that has undergone evolution, then two quite different things follow. First, the processes that have shaped human characteristics must be the same natural-selection processes that have shaped the characteristics of all species; humans, like all the other animals, must have evolved through a system of adaptation to their environment. Second, the fact of evolution implies that humans, like the other animals, have a phylogenetic past that relates them to all other living creatures. In other words, scientists can establish the evolutionary relationship of human beings to other living species by tracing the lines of descent back to common ancestors. These two ideas are respectively the *adaptive* and *historical* notions of evolutionary theory. How Darwin came to develop these revolutionary ideas will be discussed in Chapter Four.

When they were first confronted with Darwin's theory, many biologists and psychologists had already begun to reject the notion that a human being can be divided into a psychological mind or soul and a biological body. It was, consequently, a short step from their existing way of thinking to the recognition that, if the flesh of human beings has evolved, then so have their psychological capacities. And, if their psychological capacities have evolved, then the use of these capacities must have important consequences, in terms of the survival of the individual. Human psychological capacities must have specific functions. An evolutionary outlook brought about a major reorientation in the subject matter of psychology. The traditional concerns of psychology—description and analysis of the structure of the psyche, or mind—were no longer important; rather, new questions based on the intriguing notion of functional, or adaptive, evolution were asked. Psychologists, no longer content simply with an analysis of mental structure, began to question the *function* of various mental processes. How does the possession of the different capacities of mind aid in the survival of the individual? Of the species?

It is not too surprising that this "functional psychology" soon led to a concern with the individual's observable *behavior*. Studies of the adaptiveness of animals revealed that behavior is an important means by which an organism regulates its relationship to its environment. At the same time, physiologists who recognized that behavior was not really so different in kind from other functional or regulatory processes of the body began to adapt, for the study of behavior, concepts and methods that had originally been designed for the study of organ functioning. A focus on behavior not only brought the content of psychology within reach of physiology's tools but also led to the introduction of animals as tools for the understanding of human psychology.

Behavior, unlike mental structures, can be observed in the simplest as well as in the most complex of animals. This fact suggested to psychologists that they could conveniently ascertain general rules of behavior the way physiologists were already ascertaining general rules of organ functioning—by working with animals. The consequence of the functional reorientation in biological and psychological thought begun by Darwin's theory was a situation in which physiologists, at home in the study of animals, began to extrapolate to humans and in which psychologists, once confined to the vagaries of the human mind, began to add the behavior of animals to their subject matter. In this early period, it was sometimes difficult to distinguish a psychologist interested in behavior from a physiologist interested in behavior; they both aimed at understanding the mechanisms of behavior and both conceived of behavior as a regulatory, adaptive, or functional process.

It was the second, historical, notion of evolutionary theory, however, that captured the most attention among psychologists as well as among people in general. Recognition of human kinship with other living beings (a scandalous, exciting idea, discussed at the turn of the century not only in academia but also in pulpits and courtrooms) held the promise that the study of contemporary animals would yield insights into the characteristics of the phylogenetic ancestors of human beings and, hence, into basic human nature. For psychologists, the historical aspect of evolutionary theory implied that the characteristics of the human mind have phylogenetic precursors that must be observable in present-day animals. Darwin himself came to this conclusion and began the task of examining precursors of human mentality with the publication of *The Descent of Man* and *The Expression of the Emotions in Man and Animals*. Darwin was prompted to engage in this task in part by the fact that many people refused to believe that humans are involved in the evolutionary process. Darwin's purpose in writing these books was to demonstrate that all those characteristics considered unique to humans, and used to support arguments against human participation in the evolutionary process, are in fact shared by most animals.

The Anecdotalists and the Origin of Comparative Psychology

In the wake of Darwin's publications, a group of natural historians emerged, most of whom were intent on demonstrating the continuity between the human mind and the mind of animals. Their method for demonstrating this continuity was simply to collect stories or anecdotes about animals and their behavior from breeders, pet owners, and other such animal enthusiasts. The most notable of the *anecdotalists,* as they are called, was George Romanes (1848–1894), a thoroughly convinced Darwinian and an important figure in the establishment of mental evolution as a field of study. Romanes, and others of the anecdotalist school, emphasized naturalistic and descriptive studies, but the abiding concern of these theorists with the establishment of a commonality between humans and animals resulted in an anthropomorphic distortion in most of their observations, reports, and interpretations. Anthropomorphism—the attribution of human characteristics to other animals—is still very difficult to avoid and can be found even in some of the modern literature. Why is anthropomorphism so seductive, and what is wrong with it, anyway?

Animals can do many marvelous things. Consider for a moment the intricate web of a spider, the worldwide migration of birds, the complex social organization of ants, the communicative abilities of honeybees, or the behavior of your own pet. In all of these examples it can be observed that animals are able to execute highly complex tasks that serve definite purposes. The spider's web is not only a marvel of architecture; it is also designed in such a way that it will catch small insects that provide the spider's food. Honeybees have a language that not only is intricately structured but also allows them to communicate the location and type of food to other bees in the hive. Should the behaviors of the spider and the bee be considered purposeful? Is the honeybee guided by altruistic motives? When humans engage in comparably complex behavior, they are capable of perceiving and being guided by their goals. In other words, behavior in humans is purposeful in the ordinary sense of "intended." People can describe their behavior in terms of its aims and purposes, and their descriptions are obviously well understood by others. In the early stages of animal-behavior studies, especially among members of the anecdotalist movement, it was a common mistake to assume that a complex behavioral outcome implied equally complex causes and that the causes underlying complex behavior in animals are of the same order of complexity as the causes underlying complex behavior in humans. For example, it was assumed that the processes a spider goes through when building its web are similar to the processes humans would go through were they to build a similar web. These processes include having a clear conception of the relationship between the behavior and the goal and bringing to bear architectural knowledge sufficient for web construction. Thus, the spider's behavior was considered purposeful: the web is built to catch insects, and insects are caught to provide nourishment. Web-spinning was also considered thoughtful behavior, because it exhibits some of the basic principles of architectural and physical design.

Psychologists recognized that the anecdotal, anthropomorphic method was fallacious—that projections of introspectively known motives and capabilities onto animals can be in error. For example, it has been shown that the form of a cecropia silkworm's cocoon is not decided by the silkworm's purpose or knowledge but by the structure of the spinning apparatus and the properties of the local environment chosen as a spinning site. It is possible to structure the environment of this caterpillar so that it will spin but fail to spin a cocoon (Van der Kloot & Williams, 1953a, 1953b). As a means of protecting themselves against the seductive fallacy of anthropomorphism, psychologists took to heart a dictum proposed by C. Lloyd Morgan (1852–1936). This dictum, known as Morgan's Canon, advised that, if there are two or more possible explanations of something, one should always choose the simplest, even if it's not the most appealing. The simplest explanation supposes the least-complex functioning on the part of the behaving organism. Attribution of human emotions and purposes to animals is effectively precluded if this dictum is followed, since some other, simpler explanation can always be sought and can usually be found.

Perhaps because of natural historians' reliance on anecdotalism, psychologists, with some important exceptions, turned their backs on natural history. However, natural historians continued to flourish in biology and to develop some powerful conceptual and methodological tools, primarily for use in the study of natural selection. They continued to be interested in behavior, particularly as it is involved in sexual selection, and, as we shall show later, natural history reentered psychology in the mid-20th century through the discipline of ethology.

Although the natural-history method was dropped by the mainstream of psychology in favor of the experimental method, a legacy of the early post-Darwinian era was retained: the fervent belief in the basic similarity of humans and animals. In the behaviorist movement, especially as it was embodied by John B. Watson (1878–1958), the anecdotalists' contention that they could find human characteristics in animals was completely inverted. Watson insisted that psychology must stick to observables, and observable behavior is movement of muscles and secretions of glands. He followed Morgan's Canon so assiduously that complex functioning in both humans and animals was either ignored or explained in terms of simple processes, to the

point of serious distortion of the phenomena studied. Explanation of all behavior in terms of simple stimulus–response (S–R) units was the goal. All
S–R bonds were considered to be basically alike and to be formed through the
same processes. By this reasoning, the mechanism of behavior is the same in
all species; differences between organisms and between species lie merely in
the content or quantity of S–R bonds. Watson, a psychologist, thought he had
achieved the physiologists' goal of formulating general laws of behavior. To
be fair, we must note that the young Watson was often cautious and restrained
in his explanations of behavior. Although he is often portrayed as a simplistic
radical environmentalist, a careful examination of his work reveals contributions, such as naturalistic studies of animals, that extend beyond this narrow
framework.

Some Early Conceptions of Psychological Development

Before the behaviorist movement, the systematic study of babies and
small children was not possible in psychology. No methods were available for
use with these nonverbal creatures other than anecdotal descriptions of their
innocence or depravity. Once behavior was admitted as a fitting subject matter, however, it became as possible to study the preverbal human as it was to
study animals or adult humans. Watson found that the concepts and methods
that he had championed for the study of animal behavior were also quite
suitable for the study of infants and toddlers. After his early work with
animals, therefore, he turned his attention to the study of children and began a
new trend in developmental psychology.

The history of developmental psychology did not begin with the
behaviorists, however; several earlier theoretical approaches to child development can be found. The oldest conception of development—*preformationism*—is that there is no development in the sense of qualitative change:
everything is formed from the beginning. Those people now automatically
thought of as children were in this conception thought of simply as small
versions of human beings. Adults and children played the same games, did
similar work, and wore similar clothes. The only difference was that children,
not having experienced as much, did not know as much. Representations of
children in paintings characteristic of this period look to us today like minia-
ture adults (Aries, 1962). Were the features that strike us so immediately as
characteristics of children, rather than of adults, perceived at all?

Conceptually, preformationism is in the tradition of instantaneous
creation and original sin. The ultimate moment for this doctrine occurred
when someone looked at a human sperm under the newly invented microscope
and saw, inside the sperm, a tiny but perfectly featured human being. This
vision was drawn, reproduced in textbooks, and dutifully seen (except by

those who argued that the homunculus was in the ovum) by others who looked at sperm through microscopes—at least for a while.

The methodology of preformationist theories consisted of casual armchair observations and philosophical reflections, much like the anecdotal method of the early students of animal behavior. Like the anecdotalists, the armchair developmentalists were committed to a projective mode of thinking. There were no precise observational and experimental methods available at this time, and their recourse was to project explanations devised for a privately known existence (thoughts, feelings, purposes, and so on) onto others, including children.

Because people's views of themselves change, the projections they make also change. With a change in the intellectual climate, preformationism was replaced by another way of conceiving of development: *predeterminism*. The predeterminist movement began to grow in strength during the 19th century, gaining support from popular demands for sociopolitical reform and from the change in intellectual climate fostered by a general acceptance of Darwin's theory of evolution. Largely through the pen of Rousseau, people became aware of development in the sense of qualitative change during the life span. Children were perceived as smiling, fat-cheeked cherubs. The idea of original sin fell into disfavor. "Savages," supposedly free from the obstacles of civilization, were seen as noble and pure—the perfect products of a cherubic beginning.

In the predeterminist scheme, development is an orderly and preordained progression through a series of distinct stages. The goal of this progression is a good and perfect person, and, as this end is predetermined, it can best be achieved in a supportive, nurturant, and permissive environment—not an interactive one. Hence, whereas savages may be noble, "civilized" people—people who live under a system of social and political restrictions—cannot be.

Because Darwin's theory was designed to account for diversity and continuity among the various life forms, and because development within a single life span also exhibits change and continuity, some of those attempting to understand development looked to the notion of evolution for useful explanations of individual development. The embryologists—notably, Haeckel (1834–1919)—arrived at the idea that the series of highly orderly and predictable qualitative changes observable in the form and functioning of embryos were reflections of progressive changes in the phylogenetic past of that embryo. That is, they hypothesized that an embryo retraces in abbreviated form during its development all of the evolutionary changes that its ancestors have gone through. This is Haeckel's law: ontogeny recapitulates phylogeny.

G. Stanley Hall (1846–1924) borrowed the recapitulation notion from embryology and applied it to the postembryonic psychological functioning of the developing person. The predeterminist's conception of development as a series of qualitatively different stages occurring in a preestablished and invariant sequence and having a predetermined end point was thereby both explained and supported by reference to the theory of evolution.

The predeterministic view of children, and of development, was based on the same flawed methodology used by the preformationists. Anecdotal descriptions were used, usually derived from casual observation or from an adult's memory of his or her childhood. One of the more advanced, and certainly the most popular, means of gathering developmental information was the baby biography—a narrative account of the progressive achievements of a baby, usually kept by a parent. Unfortunately, this source of information was either openly derived from or subtly influenced by the projections of the parent.

The behaviorist movement established a methodology that allowed psychologists, for the first time, actually to investigate the developing organism experimentally. Along with introducing animals into their laboratories at the beginning of this century, psychologists began to look, as scientists, at babies and children. This was certainly an essential first step toward an understanding of human development. Unfortunately, however, the behaviorist movement, particularly as it was interpreted by Watson, brought to psychology an extreme *environmentalist* viewpoint. The commitment to this outlook had the effect of preventing psychologists from understanding the phenomenon of qualitative change articulated by such predeterminists as Hall. This extreme environmentalism constituted, in effect, a denial—although a denial quite different from that of the preformationists—of the existence of development. As we pointed out earlier, Watson held that the only real difference between one species and another is in number and content of S–R bonds. He applied this formula to the differences in the same organism at different points in the life span. A young child could thus be said to possess all the same psychological capacities as an adult, because all these capacities can be reduced to the formation of simple S–R units. Development, then, is merely a quantitative affair; the only ''stages'' one needs in order to describe development are immaturity (the learning stage) and maturity (the learned stage) (see Bijou & Baer, 1961).

To many people—especially those committed to the environmentalist position—developmental psychology is the same thing as child psychology. Developmental psychology involves more than an examination of the child, however. Development is a life-span process, the understanding of which requires empirical knowledge of the specific factors responsible for each particular developmental transition or trend. The environmentalists tend not to search for these factors but rather to assume that they are the same, for any stage or for any organism, as those governing change of behavior in specific learning experiments conducted with adult rats, pigeons, or humans. When working with children, adults, or senior citizens, environmentalists seem interested mainly in demonstrating that the same contrived situation will modify all these subjects' behavior in much the same way. Any of the more complex phenomena of developmental transitions are assumed to be mere extensions of the factors effecting these simple changes. Recent evidence from other researchers, however, has brought seriously into question this simplistic environmentalist position, even for its most "firmly" established phenomena (Hinde & Stevenson-Hinde, 1973; Schneirla, 1966; Seligman, 1970).

As we have shown in this brief historical sketch, developmental and comparative psychology converged in the early 20th century. They became accepted, and even popular, parts of mainstream psychology, but from our point of view this phase in their development was rather pedestrian and fruitless. Developmental psychologists occupied themselves primarily with establishing age norms in children, and comparative psychologists studied learning in white rats. Exciting undercurrents were kept alive in both disciplines, however, and developmental psychology, again in a manner parallel with that of comparative psychology, has enjoyed a new, vigorous growth in the past 20 or so years. Much of this new growth has been nurtured by recent developments within biology.

Summary

In this chapter we have argued that psychology should be considered an aspect of biology rather than a separate discipline. However, we noted that psychology and biology have been separated by traditions of training that have provided students with different methods, techniques, interests, and aims. These differences have inevitably led to problems for people attempting interdisciplinary study by leading to the distortion by each discipline of concepts borrowed from the other. We used the concept of imprinting to illustrate this problem. Finally, we briefly sketched the history of two subdivisions of psychology—developmental psychology and comparative psychology—showing their common origin in Darwin's theory of evolution and their influence on each other's development. In the next chapter we will describe four specific philosophical problems plaguing the integration of biology and psychology.

Chapter Two

Biology and Psychology: Problems for a Synthesis

Psychology and biology have converged at many different points in their histories, and both have grown as a result. However, there are a few persistent problems that emerge, in one guise or another, whenever one tries to synthesize an interdisciplinary approach from the two. The problems stem from some of the positions that have been taken on the issue of the relationship of biology to psychology. Four interrelated but separable positions have been most common: (1) *a hierarchical conception of science*, (2) *reductionism*, (3) *culture–biology dualism*, and (4) *the biological imperative*. We feel that these four widely endorsed positions create serious problems for a psychobiology of development.

The Hierarchy of Science

One of the most pervasive conceptions of science is that there is some natural hierarchical ordering among scientific disciplines. In this scheme, each discipline is dependent on the achievements of the discipline below it. Physics is the most basic science, followed by, in order, chemistry, biology, psychology, sociology, and so on. This order appears so natural that, for example, people often talk of the psychological basis of sociology but do not speak seriously of the sociological basis of psychology.

Acceptance of the hierarchical notion, whether implicit or explicit, can lead psychologists to conceive of the relationship between psychology and biology—and especially between psychology and the fields of physiology and molecular biology—as one in which biological knowledge forms the basis for psychological knowledge, but never the reverse. That is, concepts, laws, and theories of physiology are considered important sources for the formation of the concepts, laws, and theories of psychology. Psychology, however, is thought to play no formative role in physiology; at best, psychology can only provide new problems to be solved by physiologists. "The biological basis of behavior," or some similar phrase, appears in virtually every psychology textbook, which indicates the extent of the acceptance of this belief.

A hierarchical conception of science also has implications for the way in which scientists think about themselves and about their colleagues. The more fundamental a science, the more powerful its explanations, and thus the better it is—or so the thinking goes. This reasoning leads to a state of affairs in which certain physiologists and other biologists feel free to ignore developments within psychology and in which certain psychologists consider themselves somehow less scientific than their biological colleagues, whom they strive to emulate. It is not at all uncommon for biologists, chemists, or physicists who are quite naïve with respect to psychology to write on the subject matter of psychology and to have their work accorded the status of an expert's, even by psychologists. The reverse is rare or nonexistent.[1] The same social dynamics frequently lead psychologists to adopt the trappings of their colleagues in physiology; psychology laboratories abound in the latest physiological equipment, and psychology journals are filled with physiology jargon. To be sure, much of this activity is in the service of furthering the understanding of behavior, but one suspects that at least some of the motivation has more to do with promoting the feeling of status in the psychologist than with answering psychological questions.

One disturbing consequence of the view that biology and psychology are hierarchically related is that the discovery that some piece of behavior is genetically influenced, or correlated with the activity of a particular area of the brain, or dependent on the presence of some particular chemical has the effect of ending psychological inquiry. The behavior is presumed to be as understood as psychologists can make it. Further elucidation of the phenomenon is then left to the experts at a more basic level of the scientific pyramid. Yet many significant advances in the understanding of behavior have come from inversions in this hierarchy of science.

Some Inversions of Biology and Psychology in the Hierarchy of Science

Genes and behavior. A good illustration of the importance of psychological investigation for furthering the understanding of "biologically based" phenomena concerns the relationship between genetic and developmental analyses of behavior. The behavior geneticist is interested primarily in

---

[1]Of course, there are many individuals, biologists by training, who are quite sophisticated in the psychological literature, and vice versa. We do not wish to imply that one ought to stay within the bounds of one's own discipline—only that such trespassing shouldn't be done without extensive knowledge of the terrain.

characterizing the relationship between individual genetic differences and differences in behavior among the members of some population or group. The developmentalist is interested primarily in ascertaining the conditions of ontogeny necessary for the occurrence of some behavior or behavioral change in the individual. Unfortunately, it is often assumed that a genetic analysis of behavior can substitute for a developmental analysis. Two studies of the behavior of mice nicely illustrate the importance of distinguishing between the genetic and developmental approaches to behavior.

A common mode of demonstrating genetic influences on behavior involves rearing two or more inbred strains[2] of mice in virtually identical environments. The differences between the strains on some behavioral measure, such as fighting or visual exploration, are presumed to result from the genetic differences between the strains. In an elegant series of studies, Ressler (1963) investigated the development of the differences in adult weight and visual exploration between two strains of mice—one with white fur (BALB/c) and the other with black fur (C57BL/10). Ressler began his developmental studies with the knowledge that, even when the two strains are reared in the same highly controlled laboratory conditions and given access to the same amount of food, the white mice are significantly heavier and more exploratory as adults than the black mice.

Initially, Ressler cross-fostered the young of both strains immediately after birth. That is, white-strain foster parents raised black young, and black-strain foster parents raised white young. When tested as adults, black mice that had been raised by white foster parents were significantly heavier and more exploratory than either white or black mice raised by black foster parents. In other words, genetically black mice raised for the first 21 days after birth by white foster parents showed adult behavioral and weight characteristics similar to those of genetically white mice raised by white foster parents, and white mice reared by black foster parents exhibited adult traits characteristic of black mice reared by black foster parents.

Subsequent study showed that the genetic differences in behavior between the strains are mediated, in part, by differences in parental care. White foster parents lick, groom, and carry the young more than black foster parents. Such early stimulation has been shown to be an important influence on the ''adjustment'' of the hormonal and metabolic systems involved in the manifestation of adult weight and exploratory behavior in many mammals (Levine, 1969). Ressler (1962) also observed that the strain of the young influences the amount of ''handling'' and stimulation provided by either strain of foster parent. That is, genetically white young elicit more handling behavior from both white and black foster parents than black young. Thus, in animals that typically exhibit some sort of parental care, the gene–behavior

---

[2]An inbred strain is a population of animals all of which have the same genes. Such a strain is the result of many generations of brother–sister matings.

relationship can be clarified by detailed study of the developmental course and of the consequences of these social/behavioral experiences. Indeed, even differences in the prenatal environment of the mother's womb can significantly affect the adult behavioral characteristics exhibited by two strains of mice (DeFries, Weir, & Hegmann, 1967). Daily physical stress (swimming and noise, for instance) throughout the latter half of pregnancy in two strains of mice was found to produce offspring whose level of activity in an open field was a function of both fetal and maternal genotypes. That is, the mothers of one strain responded differently from the mothers of the other strain to the physical stress, and their reactions interacted with the genotype of the fetuses to produce adults that differed in exploratory tendencies and fearfulness.

The developmental effects of differential care can even be transmitted across more than one generation. For example, both white and black mice were found to be more exploratory if their *grandmothers* had been of the white strain than if their grandmothers had been of the black strain of mice. Thus, the differences in parental environment provided by black and white parents so affected the behavioral development of the young they reared that, when these young became mothers, they interacted with their offspring in a manner similar to the way their foster parents had interacted with them. When these offspring, in turn, became adults, their behavioral characteristics were more like those of their foster grandparents' strain than like those of their own *genetic* strain! Thus, social/environmental experience can have effects across generations via its effect on the developmental psychobiology of the organism.

The black strain has also been reported to be a highly aggressive strain that can easily be trained to fight strangers. However, Cairns (1972b) was not able to train them to fight in his laboratory. Careful comparison of the rearing conditions in his laboratory with those in which fighting has been observed revealed the source of the differences in fighting behavior. Apparently, this "highly aggressive" strain can be trained to fight strangers only if its members are reared in individual isolation cages for at least three to four weeks before testing. Cairns had inadvertently left out this essential phase of the training and reared several mice in each cage right up until the time of testing, thereby producing mice who would not fight.

Subsequent observation of these group-reared mice revealed that the mice spent little time being aggressive and a lot of time clumped together in small heaps. Clumping together apparently allowed the animals to become accustomed to the stimulation provided by other mice, even strangers. Indeed, detailed behavioral analysis of the mice in the fighting arena showed that isolation-reared mice are more likely to investigate vigorously and to explore their partner and are more intensely reactive to the stimulation provided by their partner's exploratory investigation of them than are group-reared mice. These two factors ensure that the isolation-reared animals will "become entrapped in an escalating relationship" (Cairns, 1972b, p. 397). That is, as their exploration elicits responses from their partner, the mice become even more vigorous in their exploration of the partner, until the interaction escalates into a fight.

Genes do influence behavior, but in complex animals the pathway by which genes influence behavior includes the important developmental consequences of an individual's interaction with a social and physical environment. Moreover, developmental and genetic analyses provide different, possibly complementary, perspectives on the organization of behavior. Most often the genetic analysis of behavior sets up intriguing problems to be resolved by developmental investigations. Therefore, the discovery that a behavioral pattern can be influenced by genetic manipulations should be viewed more as a beginning of psychological inquiry than as the end.

In a purely ideal sense, the notion of a hierarchy of science may have some validity. However, given the rather immature state of biology and psychology as scientific disciplines, the only supportable position concerning their relationship is that advancement in either discipline will be instrumental in the development of the other. Neither the language of biology nor the language of psychology is so rigorously developed that the statements of one can be basic to the statements of the other. Therefore, just as new developments in biology can modify purely psychological conceptions, so too can new developments in psychology modify purely biological conceptions.

Hormones and behavior.   Modern endocrinology takes as its focus understanding of the relationship between the functioning of the pituitary gland and the functioning of the nervous system. That is, endocrinology has become, largely, neuroendocrinology. The pituitary, sometimes called the "master gland" because its secretions control the functioning of so many other important glands, is located just beneath the brain. It is a small structure having two major, functionally separate lobes—anterior and posterior. The posterior lobe of the pituitary is connected to the brain by a stalk containing the axons of neurosecretory nerve cells that originate in the brain and terminate within the gland. Hormones secreted by the posterior lobe are involved in relative constriction of blood vessels, smooth-muscle contraction, and milk letdown, all of which can be stimulated by tactile, olfactory, visual, and auditory experience. Hormones secreted by the anterior lobe are involved in the regulation of growth, metabolism, and sexual physiology, among other processes. Although there is a rich network of blood vessels between the brain and the anterior pituitary, there is no neural connection between them. Consequently, endocrinologists long considered the anterior pituitary an endogenously regulated structure, with its hormonal secretions unaffected by the neurological functioning of the organism.

Geoffrey Harris (1955), in a series of elegant experiments, proved that the brain exerts control over the functioning of the anterior pituitary. By interrupting and reestablishing the blood connection between brain and an-

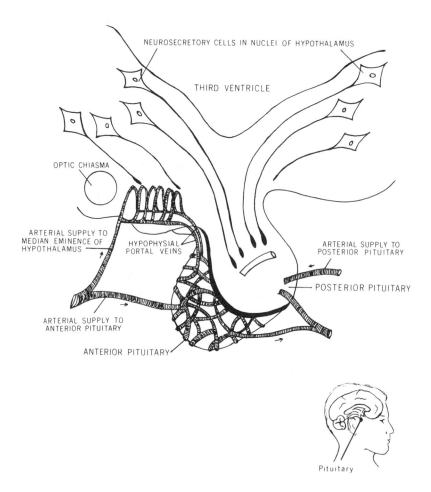

Figure 2–1. The pituitary gland is a small structure attached by a stem to the floor of the brain (see insert). The pituitary's posterior lobe has a neural connection with the hypothalamus and is important in systems requiring rapid delivery of hormones. The anterior pituitary secretes trophic hormones into the blood. These hormones have many functions, including the control of such other glands as testis, ovary, and adrenal cortex. There is no neural connection between the brain and the anterior pituitary, but the brain controls the functioning of the anterior pituitary nonetheless, with neurosecretions that travel from the median eminence of the hypothalamus through the rich hypophyseal portal network to the secretory cells of the anterior pituitary. Adapted from *General Endocrinology* (6th ed.), by C. D. Turner and J. T. Bagnara. Copyright 1976 by W. B. Saunders Company. Used by permission.

terior pituitary, he and his colleagues showed that substances essential for pituitary regulation are secreted within the brain. These neurosecretory substances, called *releasing factors*, travel via blood vessels to the anterior pituitary, where they regulate the secretory activity of the cells. The secretions of the cells of the anterior pituitary are emptied into the general systemic circulation and quickly reach their target organs. Other endocrine glands, such as the thyroid, gonads, and adrenals, depend on the hormones produced by the anterior pituitary for their normal functioning.

Long before Harris demonstrated the mechanism by which the brain exerts its control over the pituitary, there was behavioral evidence to indicate that the nervous system is involved in the control of the endocrine system. The work of Rowan (1931) and Marshall (1936), for example, had shown that the annual gonadal cycles of hormonal secretion in birds are controlled by changes in day length and other external stimuli. This, and other behavioral evidence, strongly implied that the nervous system must provide the link between endocrine-system functioning and changes in the environment. However, it was several decades before endocrinologists arrived at the understanding of endocrine-system regulation achieved earlier by scientists focusing on the behavior of animals.

Interestingly, the notion that hormones can affect behavior has been subscribed to by scientists since antiquity. It has repeatedly been observed that castration—of domestic animals, for example—frequently leads to behavioral changes. During the 1930s and 1940s, scientists began systematically to study the relationship between hormones and behavior by applying such standard endocrinological techniques as gland removal and injection of glandular extracts. It was found that hormones do indeed affect behaviors, ranging from sexual performance to care of the young, aggression, social relations, and even, in many species, the ability to learn quickly (Beach, 1948; Levine, 1972). The fact that nervous-system involvement in behavior is so pervasive led researchers interested in the relationship between hormones and behavior to hypothesize that hormones operate by affecting neural functioning. Evidence directly supporting this hypothesis was obtained by means of a synthesis of the methodologies of neurology and endocrinology—disciplines within physiology heretofore quite separate from each other. For example, instead of injecting hormones into the general blood supply, researchers implanted tiny amounts of crystalline hormones in circumscribed areas of the brain. As a result, two important discoveries were made: first, that hormones can affect behavior centrally by altering the activity of brain cells involved in the performance of the behavior and, second, that there are brain cells that monitor the level of hormones in the blood, thus serving as an essential link in the feedback control of the endocrine system. For example, androgen is maintained at a relatively constant level in many male vertebrates because the brain produces gonadotrophin releasing factors when androgen drops below a certain level and stops producing them when circulating androgen rises above a certain level. Thus, the nervous system is a "target organ" for many hormones.

The endocrine system and the nervous system are mutually dependent systems, and understanding of either of them is aided by a neuroendocrinological approach. Although many factors were involved in the development of neuroendocrinology as a science, a convincing argument can be made that this advance in physiology owes much to antecedent advances in the study of behavior—in particular, to developments in the study of hormones and behavior. Indeed, work on hormone–behavior relationships has continued to develop, with researchers using psychological terms and concepts for which there are no available physiological translations.

Consider, for example, the reproductive cycle of the ring dove, which consists of a series of both behavioral and hormonal changes. Lehrman and his students (for example, Lehrman, 1965, 1971) have shown that the behavioral transition from nest-building to incubation is facilitated by the secretion of progesterone, which operates in conjunction with either estrogen or androgen. The secretion of progesterone is, in turn, facilitated by the dove's participation in both courtship and nest-building activities. Shortly after incubation begins, prolactin—the hormone responsible for the development of cropmilk—begins to be secreted from the dove's anterior pituitary. *Cropmilk* is the protein-rich substance formed from the cells lining the inner surface of the dove's crop—a part of its digestive system. The parent doves feed this substance to their young during the first few days after the squabs have hatched.

Prolactin has been shown to be ineffective in the initiation of incubation, but, once incubation has started, prolactin is responsible for the maintenance of incubation and for the rapid transition of the dove to care of the young after they've hatched. Interestingly, prolactin is secreted in response to the tactile stimulation received from the nest and eggs during incubation and to the visual stimulation of observing an incubating mate! However, the secretion of prolactin in response to the observation of an incubating mate can occur only in doves that have had the opportunity to initiate incubation before being separated from the nest and eggs.

Although it may be relatively easy to translate into neuroendocrinological terms the fact that a ring dove will secrete prolactin in response to stimulation from its nest and eggs or the fact that progesterone injected into doves will induce them to incubate eggs, it is not so easy to translate the equally evident fact that ring doves must be under particular *experiential* conditions before they will secrete prolactin in response to stimulation from the nest, eggs, and mate or before they will incubate in response to progesterone. Indeed, the understanding of this experiential aspect of the neuroendocrine system is far more advanced on a psychological level of investigation than on the physiological level. For this reason, Lehrman chose to emphasize the psychological dimension in his description of the psychobiological organization of the ring-dove reproductive cycle.

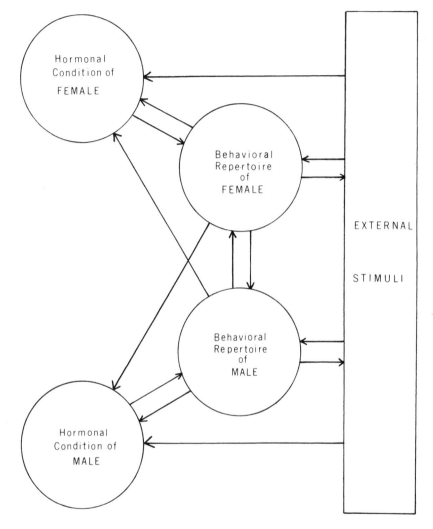

Figure 2–2. As the arrows indicate, the hormonal condition of many animals, including ring doves, is affected by the animal's own behavior, by the behavior of a social partner, and by the physical environment. Social and physical environments coact with hormones to affect behavior. As you can see, the relationships among hormones, behavior, and stimuli are complex, involving indirect and reciprocal pathways. For example, the hormonal condition of the male, by affecting his behavior, can affect the hormonal condition of the female. The study of behavior is thus necessary to an understanding of neuroendocrinology.

The regulation of the reproductive cycle of the ring dove appears to depend, at least in part, on a double set of reciprocal interrelations. First, there is an interaction of the effects of hormones on behavior and the effects of external stimuli—including those that arise from the behavior of the animal and its mate—on the secretion of hormones. Second, there is a complicated reciprocal relation between the effects of the presence and behavior of one mate on the endocrine system of the other and the effects of the presence and behavior of the second bird (including those aspects of its behavior induced by these endocrine effects) back on the endocrine system of the first. The occurrence in each member of the pair of a cycle found in neither bird in isolation, and the synchronization of the cycles in the two mates, can now readily be understood as consequences of this interaction of the inner and outer environments [Lehrman, 1964, p. 54].[3]

Learning and the autonomic nervous system.   Another illustration of the importance of psychological investigation to the advancement of physiology is the work Miller (1969) and his students have done on the functioning of the autonomic nervous system. The autonomic nervous system consists of two separable systems—sympathetic and parasympathetic—which are involved in the rapid regulation of general systemic functions, such as blood pressure, kidney functioning, and heart rate. Neurologists long operated under the assumption that neither system could be brought under voluntary control (that is, control of the brain) and that, in addition, the sympathetic system responded as a unit. In other words, the functions regulated by the sympathetic nervous system, such as constriction of blood vessels, could not occur in some areas of the body and not in others. Using the psychological knowledge that responses can be increased, decreased, separated, or attached to other responses, according to their association with positive reinforcement, Miller proved that the autonomic nervous system can be brought under the control of the brain and that the functions of the sympathetic system can be carried out on a local level. First, it was found that a rat would learn to perform a response in order to receive electrical stimulation of certain areas of its brain. Miller then made stimulation of these areas contingent on some autonomic response, such as an increase or decrease in heart rate, lowered blood pressure in one ear accompanied by raised blood pressure in the other, or an increase or decrease in the amount of water the kidney extracts from the blood. The rats were able to effect the necessary changes. Because many health problems, such as hypertension and coronary problems, reflect autonomic-nervous-system functioning, Miller has argued that his results with rats broaden the scope and foundation of psychosomatic medicine. His results suggest not only that ''cures'' may be sought through ''biofeedback'' and reinforcement but also that it may be possible to determine the etiology of many health problems by examining the social-reinforcement environment of the patient.

[3]From "The Reproductive Behavior of Ring Doves," by D. S. Lehrman, *Scientific American,* 1964, *211,* pp. 48–54. Reprinted by permission.

These examples of psychology's importance in the development of biological disciplines are significant not only because they illustrate the relationship between psychology and biology but also because they are directly relevant to the construction of a developmental psychobiology. Each of these examples focuses on psychobiological principles important in the behavioral development of humans and other animals. Human behavior, as well as that of animals, involves a complex of reciprocal interactions between the individual's endocrine and neurological conditions and its social and physical environmental experiences. It is the changing nature of these relationships during ontogeny that attracts the interest of the developmental psychobiologist.

Reductionism

The conception of a hierarchy of science is closely allied to the notion of reductionism. Indeed, reductionism assumes a hierarchy of scientific disciplines, at least with respect to explanatory scope. Reductionism, simply stated, is the idea that the postulates, laws, and hypotheses of one discipline can be completely translated into the postulates, laws, and hypotheses of another discipline. Furthermore, it is assumed that this translation results in a simpler, more fundamental explanation of events.

Reductionism rests on the widely shared belief that nature is all of one piece. If, as implied by the hierarchical view of science, any discipline can be reduced to the next lower discipline, it follows that all scientific disciplines can ultimately be reduced to one basic science. Thus, a reductionist might argue that, since psychological processes are relatively high-order phenomena, the proper way to understand them is to translate them into progressively more elemental processes. Although the ultimate aim may be to achieve a physicochemical explanation, in practice reductionistic psychologists usually move only to the level of a physiological or anatomical analysis. Traditionally, this has resulted in explanations of psychological phenomena in terms of the structure and functioning of the nervous system and, more recently, in neurobiochemical terms. Explication of the physiological or biochemical mechanism that is characteristic of some psychological event is considered the explanation of that event. To a reductionist, *the best explanation is the one that spells out the mechanism in the greatest detail or that achieves the greatest reduction toward the most "elemental" laws of science.*

Along with the reductionists, we can agree that there is unity in nature and that there is unity in science. We can also agree that it may be possible, at least in theory, to translate all phenomena into terms of physics and chemistry and that such translations may constitute explanations. However, we would pause to argue that for some purposes reductionism has little or no explanatory value or may be totally beside the point and that in these cases it is more an intellectual exercise than a scientific technique. The value of an explanation is determined, in part, by its appropriateness to the question being asked, and, as we will argue in the next chapter, there are a variety of qualitatively different questions that may be asked about behavior, each with a different use and each answerable in a qualitatively different way. The important distinctions among questions can be lost through reduction. Moreover, when an explanation constructed at one level of complexity is reduced to more elemental terms, some sources for understanding may be lost. This is particularly true either when the phenomena to be reduced are not clearly defined or identified or when the level to which they will be reduced is as yet relatively unexplored. As we indicated earlier, neither biology or psychology is a rigorous enough discipline for a proper reduction of psychology to the terms of biology to occur. Finally, the reductionist hypothesis does not imply a "constructionist" one (P. W. Anderson, 1972). Even if one could reduce psychological phenomena, concepts, and laws to the more "fundamental" concepts and laws of physics, chemistry, or biology, one would not necessarily be able to construct the phenomena, concepts, and laws of psychology from physics, chemistry, or biology. As phenomena and events become more complex, involving more components, entirely new properties appear, the understanding of which cannot be achieved by means of a reductionist perspective.

The Distinction between Necessary and Sufficient Conditions

It is sometimes argued by reductionists that, unless a psychological construct can be related to a physiological event, it has no validity; once related to some biological fact, the psychological construct has been explained. Unfortunately, this argument tends to ignore the distinction between necessary and sufficient conditions. A necessary condition is one that must be present if a phenomenon or event is to occur, whereas a sufficient condition is one the presence of which always initiates the phenomenon or event. This distinction is particularly relevant to an understanding of the relationship between the anatomical and physiological characteristics of the nervous system and behavioral development.

Like the study of biochemistry, the study of the anatomy and physiology of the nervous system can be a thoroughly fascinating and somewhat seductive scientific endeavor. With modern techniques, the different structural components of the nervous system can be teased apart and their physiological characteristics identified. Ever-more-sophisticated techniques can be used to examine the ultrastructure and functioning of individual cells. There are billions of cells, with myriad interconnections, to arouse our admiration. Besides this diversity of components, the nervous system also exhibits a precise regularity in its structural organization. It is this structural organization that has attracted the most experimental attention from physiologically oriented psychologists. Their results generally reveal correlations between the presence and activity of certain components of the nervous system and presence of specific behaviors.

The discovery of correlations between neuroanatomy and behavior have particularly interested developmental psychologists interested in humans. Given that the human nervous system continues to develop for at least 10 to 18 years after birth, might not developmental changes in behavior during this period be the consequence of maturational changes in the nervous system? This question has generated a good deal of discussion, especially among psychologists interested in the development of language skills.

Several theorists have argued that the syntactic nature of language precludes its acquisition through traditional learning techniques. *Syntax* refers to the rule system used both to describe the way words can be arranged into appropriate sentence constructions and to understand how different sentences are related. Because these rules are not readily apparent in adult speech, because adults typically are not able to describe these rules, and because children exhibit in their speech all of the basic characteristics of syntax by age 3, it is argued that the child's acquisition of language cannot be achieved by any known learning process. Typically, it is concluded that humans must possess some innate forms of knowledge of language. One feature of language that has been used to prove or illustrate its innateness is its "biological basis." The strongest evidence for this biological basis comes from the study of brain-damaged children and adults.

In the mid-19th century, Paul Broca discovered that damage to a particular area of the left side of an adult's brain resulted in loss of normal speech (aphasia). Later in the same century, Carl Wernicke observed that damage to a different part of this left cerebral hemisphere (Wernicke's area) also resulted in a language disorder. In Wernicke's patients, however, language was not slow and telegraphic as in Broca's aphasia but rather rapid, well articulated, grammatical, and devoid of content. Persons with Broca's aphasia are able to understand language but have difficulty in speaking, whereas persons with Wernicke's aphasia have no difficulty in speaking but cannot comprehend their own speech or the speech of others! Wernicke went on to suggest that, because Broca's area is adjacent to the region of the brain that controls the speech muscles, Broca's area is responsible for the coordination of these muscles. He further suggested that, because Wernicke's area is adjacent to the region of the brain involved in the processing of auditory stimulation, Wernicke's area is responsible for the comprehension of heard speech. Moreover, others hypothesized (Geschwind, 1970) that proper speech depends on the anatomical connection between these two areas. Recently it has been argued that the anatomical connection of Wernicke's area with the visual cortex through a neural complex called the *angular gyrus* is responsible for the successful comprehension of written language (Geschwind, 1970).

Because adult language functions depend on the left half of the brain,

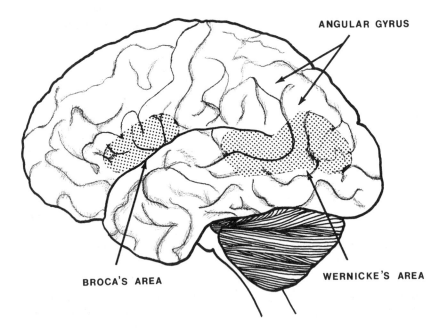

Figure 2–3. Damage to a part of the left cerebral cortex known as Broca's area results in loss of normal speech. Damage to Wernicke's area of the left cerebral cortex leads to loss of speech comprehension. The angular gyrus connects Wernicke's area with the visual cortex and may be important for comprehension of written language.

because some anatomical differences between the left and right hemispheres of the brain are evident at birth, and because changes in the child's language abilities are correlated with neuroanatomical changes in the brain, it is easy to assume that the innate syntactical character of language is the result of the development of specific brain structures. That is, the study of the causes of language development can be reduced to an understanding of the development of the brain—development that, in turn, is "fixed" by a specific genetic "blueprint." Such an assumption confuses necessary and sufficient conditions, however. The simple development of these brain structures has never been shown to initiate language development. The facts we have outlined, about the relationship of brain structure to language suggest something about the necessary conditions for language development, but they leave unanswered the question of whether there are other necessary conditions, and they indicate nothing about the processes whereby the necessary conditions become sufficient (see Ryan, 1974). Moreover, studies of language development in individuals receiving brain damage early in life reveal a greater recovery of function than would be expected if the functioning of specific areas of the left hemisphere were truly a necessary condition for language.

The Usefulness of Reductionism

Philosophically, although the fact is often overlooked in actual practice, neither reductionism nor the conception of a hierarchy of science precludes the development, at each level of science, of concepts unique to that level. Moreover, reductionism can be a useful technique for resolving questions raised by alternative positions within a given level of science that do not appear to be resolvable on that level. A good case in point concerns the alternative positions about the development of sex roles and sexual identity in humans. No amount of psychological study seems exclusively to support the psychoanalytic, the cognitive, or the social-learning position. Psychobiological examinations of the development of sex-related behavior in animals suggest that components of all three positions are relevant to an understanding of the human condition (see Money & Ehrhardt, 1972; Moore, 1977). Finally, although reductionism may be inappropriate at this stage of the scientific development of biology and psychology, a joint psychology/biology language may not be. Indeed, some philosophers of science have suggested that successful reduction of one scientific discipline to another depends on the incorporation, by *each* discipline, of the notions, concepts, laws, and phenomena of the other (Hull, 1972).

Culture–Biology Dualism

The contemporary belief in the dual nature of culture and biology is a curious combination of reductionism, a hierarchical conception of science, and the ancient belief that the mind and body are two separate kinds of *stuff*. Unlike reductionism, culture–biology dualism is not a philosophical position that has been explicitly stated and then defended by scientists. It is, rather, an attitude, an approach—a "logic-in-use" (Kaplan, 1964)—that characterizes the work of a large number of scientists engaged in examining the relationship between culture and biology. Some of the flavor of this attitude is captured by such popular phrases as "basic biological nature," "what we are really like," and "cultural veneer." A biological core overlaid with culture is the image that most frequently comes to mind.

The Assumptions Underlying Culture–Biology
Dualism

Because the dualistic position we wish to examine is to be found not in a set of stated postulates but rather in the manner in which research is conducted and interpreted, it is necessary to examine, first, some of the implicit assumptions behind such research and, second, some of the methodological limitations of the research procedures that have been used.

Culture and biology are separable. The primary assumption is that there are biological and cultural components of individuals that are both conceptually and empirically separable. The two sorts of components are different in kind and develop through different means and by different scientific principles. Biological components develop through means traditionally studied by biology, perhaps through an unfolding or a "readout" of DNA-coded information, as claimed by predeterminists, whereas cultural components develop through a process of learning or socialization. It is easily recognized that what is learned or instilled through socialization will of course vary with the cultural milieu within which an individual develops and, therefore, that the cultural aspects of individuals are plastic and variable. In contrast, it is felt that for each individual there is only one true set of biological components, although it is recognized that these may be distorted, repressed, or otherwise hidden by aberrant and destructive developmental events.

The implications of culture–biology dualism for developmental psychology are manifold. Because the two components of an individual develop independently, it is logically possible for them to be in harmony, irrelevant to each other, or in conflict (as they are, for example, in Freud's theory of personality development). Some behavioral scientists claim that an understanding of biology is unimportant to an understanding of human behavior, whereas others argue that much of what is important to human psychology is biologically determined. Of those who advocate biology's importance, some, focusing on undesirable human characteristics, argue that culture should be designed in such a way as to overcome, through restraints, by making available harmless outlets such as catharsis or redirection, or through selective breeding, undesirable biological properties, such as biologically determined propensity for aggressive behavior. Others, having the view that biology knows best, argue that cultures should be designed so as to establish a harmony with biology. This view is reflected in the concept of the "good" or "permissive" environment. It should be clear that what kind of culture is labeled desirable will depend on whether biological human nature is considered good or bad, desirable or undesirable.

Whether he or she considers human nature good or bad, the dualist conceives of a developmental psychobiologist as one whose primary task is to distinguish between aspects of behavior that are biologically determined and aspects that are culturally, or psychologically, determined, or, as it is sometimes put, to determine how much a particular behavioral pattern or characteristic is influenced by biology and how much by culture. It is here, in the definition of their task and in the methodology adopted by many developmental psychobiologists, that the logic-in-use of culture–biology dualism is most evident.

Multiple meanings of the word biology. Whenever a term has multiple, nonoverlapping meanings, there is the danger that its use will be misunderstood. *Biology* is such a term, especially when it is used in an explanatory fashion in such phrases as "biologically based" or "biologically determined." Biology is only a loosely unified science; there are several totally distinct questions and totally distinct methodologies encompassed by the label *biology*. By *distinct*, we mean that an answer to one question has no bearing on the answer to others and that a methodology appropriate for answering one question cannot yield answers to a second. Therefore, when a scientist asserts that a behavior pattern is biologically based, without further information one has no way of knowing in what sense the term *biological* is used. This is unfortunate; cultural determinants of behavior have been contrasted with biological determinants in many different senses of the term, but these different senses have not always been kept separate. In fact, the different meanings of *biological* have frequently been treated as equivalent, at least when contrasted with cultural aspects of individuals.

If some of the more widely cited examples of biologically based human behaviors are examined, it will be found that they are supported by such different arguments as: the behavior serves a biological function; the behavior has phylogenetic precursors; genes are involved; and physiological mechanisms have been related to the behavior. Considering these different arguments, there are two points that need emphasizing. One is that our conception of the dualistic nature of culture and biology takes on quite different meanings depending on the sense in which the term *biology* is intended. Second, the assertion that behavior is biologically based will raise radically different questions about the nature of development, depending, again, on the meaning attached to *biological*.

For example, Bowlby (1969) has argued that the attachment behavior of babies toward their caretakers functions, in an evolutionary sense, to reduce loss of the infants to predators. In other words, babies who show these behaviors are more likely to survive the attacks of predators and to reproduce than those who do not—or at least this was true during the time period in which these behaviors evolved. If Bowlby's argument is correct, this would mean that attachment is biologically based in the sense that it has evolved to serve a particular purpose. Contrasting biological and cultural functions, or assigning ultimate causation to one or the other, in this example, would be meaningful only if it were possible to predict different outcomes from cultural and biological analyses. Further, knowing whether the behavior functions for biological or for cultural purposes or both would be totally irrelevant to our understanding of the development of the behavior. It would not tell us, for example, whether the behavior develops through id gratification, through a process of secondary reinforcement, through perceptual learning, or through any other explanation that might be advanced. Functional analyses certainly contribute to our understanding of behavior and may aid developmental psychologists by identifying important problems for study, but, for answers to developmental questions, quite different sorts of analyses are needed.

Notions of developmental inevitability.   Lorenz (1966) has made the case that human aggression is biologically based. By this he means that the occurrence of aggression is developmentally inevitable because it represents an evolutionarily produced maturational program, or design. Evidence for his assertion comes primarily from observations that intraspecific aggression is widespread in the animal kingdom and that it is found in diverse human cultures. From a purely evolutionary perspective, his assertion creates problems that have yet to be solved. A major difficulty is the old one of distinguishing between homology and analogy. This difficulty is very great for a characteristic as ill-defined as aggression (Hinde, 1974; Klopfer, 1973). However, even if it could be unequivocally established that human aggression is homologous with aggression in other, evolutionarily related primates, or that it has phylogenetic precursors, this would tell us absolutely nothing about the development of human aggression. Homology means simply that the observed (phenotypic) similarities in aggressive behavior among the species of primates can be traced, historically, to a phenotype of a species ancestral to all the contemporary species in question. The concept of homology deals *only* with phenotypes, or developmental outcomes; therefore, it is not necessarily the case that homologous characteristics have the same underlying genes or that the characteristics have similar developmental histories (Atz, 1970; de Beer, 1958). Neither genetic nor developmental analyses are involved in the establishment of homologies. Again, questions may be raised about the developmental bases of stable characteristics, but no answers may be found by establishing phylogenies based on homologies.

The discovery that estimates of genetic differences among individuals can be related to differences in their scores on "intelligence" tests has long been assumed to identify the biological as opposed to the cultural components of intelligence (Kamin, 1974). This dualist conception prevails despite evidence showing (1) that no intelligence test could ever identify a noncultural aspect of intelligence (Ryan, 1972), (2) that the estimates of genetic differences are both inaccurate (Kamin, 1974) and inappropriate (Hirsch, 1970), and (3) that these notions of genetics have little bearing on the factors affecting the development of intelligence (Hambley, 1972). Although evidence of this sort should lead scientists and others to reject the dualistic view of intelligence, it has been either overlooked or ignored. To be sure, some of the failure to acknowledge this evidence is a consequence of the racist attitudes of certain investigators. Yet even those who reject the racist position find it hard not to believe, whether they deem it important or not, that there is some "biological core" to intelligence. As we indicated earlier, a genetic analysis of a behavior can never be a substitute for a developmental analysis. Moreover, any plasticity of problem-solving ability can be as much a biological phenomenon as any presumed fixity of this ability. Problems in education will not be resolved by being covered with smoke screens consisting of arguments about the biological nature of intelligence. Unless handicapped by severe neurological damage, all persons can develop reading, writing, and thinking skills sufficient for dealing with the complexities of modern society. That this has not yet been achieved should not be considered a sign that it cannot.

Methodological Consequences of the Dualist Assumptions

The separation of culture and biology.   If one accepts the assumptions of dualism—namely, that biological and cultural components are separable and that biological components are characterized by developmental inevitability—the first logical step in a developmental investigation is an attempt to separate the two factors. Hutt (1972), for example, has argued that human sex differences are biologically based, in the sense of deriving from neuroendocrine mechanisms, and, therefore, that they are not culturally based. Others (for example, Hampson & Hampson, 1961) have argued that human sex differences are culturally based, or learned from the social environment, and that, therefore, biological factors are irrelevant to their development. However, these two conflicting statements are based on dualistic assumptions, and, once these assumptions are rejected, the basis for the conflict may disappear. It is not necessary—in fact, it may not be possible—to begin a psychobiological analysis by separating biological from psychological components. It can be shown that the very nature of the neuroendocrine mechanism underlying sex differences depends, at least in part, on input from the social environment. Identical twins have been reared so that one exhibits characteristic female behavior and the other characteristic male behavior (Money & Ehrhardt, 1972). Further, it can be shown that the nature of the social influences encountered by a developing individual is affected by the neuroendocrine-based characteristics of that individual (Money & Ehrhardt, 1972; Moore, 1977). The logic-in-use, or the methods of inquiry and the assumption base from which conclusions are drawn from data, of contemporary investigators who seek to separate cultural from genetic and physiological determinants of behavior is indistinguishable from that of instinct theorists. It is based on the same dichotomous reasoning that has been shown to be untenable when made explicit in instinct theory (Lehrman, 1953, 1970).

Reification.   Interestingly, the belief in the duality of culture and biology did not arise as a result of research on behavior; it is a belief that preceded modern behavior study. It stems from two major sources. The first source is the reification as separate entities of our two separate ways for knowing about ourselves: introspection and observation. Reification is a potentially fallacious thought process whereby a distinction that actually characterizes our *methods of knowing about* something is treated as a real property of, or *distinction belonging to,* the object of study. Historically, people have frequently thought of a person—in fact, one single organism—as a composite of two separate things. The mind came to be that which one knows about through introspection (thinking about oneself) and the body that which one knows about through the senses. The mind–body reification was carried to its greatest extremes in religion and mythology and has even had a firm place in science. Only recently have some scientists sought to remove its influence (see, for example, Klein, 1970).

The second, and more modern, source of culture–biology dichotomy is the reification of our various scientific activities. People talk not of the *activities* of chemists, biologists, and psychologists but of the chemical, biological, or psychological *nature* of things. A split that belongs in fact to our disciplinary conception of science has been visited upon the organism. Clearly, distinctions must be made if science is to progress, but scientists must always bear in mind the referents of their categories.

Some recent developments in behavioral biology have established an interesting paradox for those who would distinguish cultural from biological aspects of behavior by reifying the activities of scientists. One of the best examples of research in this new area is the research done on the Japanese snow monkey. An ingenious juvenile monkey learned one day that sweet potatoes are better if they are washed in the ocean; this discovery was transmitted throughout the resident troop. Later, she discovered that she could wash grains of wheat, thrown on the beach by researchers, by dropping them into small pools or streams and waiting for them to rise to the surface. This information was also passed along to others. Both of these novel behavior patterns became part of the "folklore" of this monkey troop; under the watchful eyes of a research team, mothers passed their new habits on to their offspring, and culture was made (Miyadi, 1964).

Japanese-monkey culture is by no means independent of Japanese-monkey biology. If the monkeys had not been capable of carrying and manipulating objects with a hand, learning the relation between the washing act and the state of the potato, learning through observation of others, and a host of other activities, potato-washing would never have occurred. Further, the methods of incorporation into the culture and of transmission of the new pattern to succeeding generations are highly dependent on the species-typical social relations used by biologists to characterize the monkey group to which the Japanese monkey belongs.

Finally, the changes wrought in the life of the Japanese snow monkey as a result of the incorporation of a new behavior pattern into the life of this entire troop may have far-reaching effects on the biology of these members of the species. For instance, food-washing has led members of the troop to become more familiar with water. Juveniles now spend a great deal of time swimming and playing in the water, thereby developing new sensorimotor skills. Swimming, a new skill for these animals, may lead them to inhabit islands previously inaccessible to them, and swimming and diving have already led them to incorporate marine products into their diet (Kummer, 1971). Because culture may both affect and be affected by the evolutionary process, it is appropriate for biologists to concern themselves with the study of culture. From this point of view, the dichotomy between culture and biology is clearly nonsensical. Furthermore, if one's interest is in the *development* of behavior, it may be both artificial and misleading to try to separate effects stemming from cultural and biological sources.

We believe that the reification of culture and biology as separate phenomena has many problems associated with it, not the least of which is that it leads to a rejection of biology as irrelevant by those who are interested in the "cultural half" of humans and to a belief in biological imperatives on the part of those who are interested in the "biological half."

The Biological Imperative

The fourth problem facing the synthesis of biology and psychology involves a belief about the relationship of biological knowledge to the moral/political sphere of human concerns—a belief in what is known as the biological imperative. The biological imperative is firmly rooted in the culture–biology dualism and is based on the belief that biology affects behavior by *determining* it. That is, the effects of biology are inevitable and unchangeable; they must be taken into account by society and either fostered or removed, but they cannot be made to develop differently.

Biologists are now in a position to explore the behavior of organisms with a thoroughness never before attempted. As their interest in behavior continues and their technical sophistication grows, there is every reason to believe that the range of behaviors recognized as having biological causes will continue to grow. All behavior is biologically based in the sense that it is in principle understandable by biologists. In fact, there are biologists who are now studying culture; consequently, it makes perfectly good sense to argue that culture is biologically based. But to argue that all behavior is biologically based is not to argue that all behavior—or even that *any* behavior—is inevitable and unchangeable by cultural or psychological techniques or that it is not dependent on psychological or cultural circumstances for its development.

The biological imperative argues not only that biology determines but that it determines what is *best*. Biologically caused behavior is *natural*, and in the present climate of opinion natural means good—presumably for the individual, the society, and the future of the human species. In contrast, culture is thought to distort and to create unnatural behavior. In addition, culture can artificially accelerate changes in the environment, so that biologically based behavior, good at an earlier time, is no longer good. But, if all behavior, culture included, is biologically based, then this argument loses its impact.

Biological imperatives are usually invoked in discussions of issues about which there are many different opinions and that are emotionally charged. Some issues receiving attention recently are sex differences, maternal behavior, racial differences (especially in intelligence), and aggression. We would like to point out two obvious sources of fallacy in the biological-imperative argument.

The Fallacy of Value-Based Scientific Arguments

First, value-based arguments are frequently mixed up in scientific ones. The chain of thought that runs from biologically caused to natural to good can, of course, proceed in the opposite direction, especially given the extensive diversity of biological phenomena. If, for example, one favors an arrangement wherein a mother looks after her child for the first few years of life, one has only to look to find biological causes for this arrangement. To use these biological causes to argue against any alternative arrangement is to avoid the societal debate about the kind of children we wish to raise or about the roles of men and women in society.

Consider the study of attachment behavior in monkeys. A rhesus macaque is seriously disturbed by being separated from its mother, and this disturbance continues to affect its development for a long time after reunion (Spencer-Booth & Hinde, 1967). Bowlby (1969) reports that human infants in England and in the United States are disturbed, in ways that seem similar to the disturbances of the rhesus, by being separated from the mother. This disturbance in infancy may also affect later adult social relations. It is often concluded from these two sets of observations that it is a biological necessity for a human mother to spend all of her time taking care of her child.

Now, consider the observation that in different species of macaque monkeys there are striking differences in the ease with which a baby monkey can make contact with an adult other than its mother (Kaufman, 1974). For example, when its mother is removed from the troop, the infant pigtail macaque is not able to make contact with another adult and remains squealing and rocking, alone in a corner. Bonnet-macaque young, however, are able to make contact with other adults when separated from their mothers. Indeed, they receive continuous comfort from all members of the troop. Kaufman has shown that the harmful effects of mother–infant separation are alleviated in bonnet-macaque monkeys.

Mother–infant separation in England or the United States often occurs in a situation in which there is no extended family and in which it does not seem self-evident that the father ought to stay home from work to care for the child. In Samoa, however, the family is extended such that children move readily from one set of adults to another in a network of warm interpersonal relationships wider than that included in the Western nuclear family (Mead, 1928).

In light of these differences in social organization among monkey species and among human cultures, the separation data for the rhesus monkey and the "human case" take on a different appearance. Familiarity with the differences and similarities among the social organizations of monkeys and of human cultures makes it possible to conclude that "separation from a parent-figure is extremely distressing, and has important after-effects, in the absence of a social setting that makes amelioration possible" (Lehrman, 1974, p. 194). Any other conclusions about the "biological nature" of the mother–infant relationship in humans would reflect social prejudice rather than scientific consideration.

The Naturalistic Fallacy

The fact that human mother–infant relationships as they are found in the Western nuclear family may have biological causes is beside the point, for one can just as readily find biological causes for alternative relationships. A biological-imperative argument that is used to support existing arrangements commits the *naturalistic fallacy;* that is, it asserts that what exists and is familiar is natural, and what is new and different is unnatural.

The biological-imperative view of biological causation also fails to take into account the fact that biologists themselves engage in qualitatively different activities and that the phrase "biological cause" may refer to several radically different things. This view serves to prevent the understanding of the development of behavior as it asserts that *any* "biological" cause of behavior has the same implications for development: *the development is inevitable, with only one appropriate outcome!*

Summary

In this chapter we have tried to identify some of the conceptual positions that have hindered the synthesis of the psychological and biological perspectives. When carefully examined, a hierarchical conception of science and a belief in reductionism can be seen as not necessarily precluding an integration of biology and psychology that retains the basic integrity of each. The conceptual positions characterized by a belief in culture-biology dualism and in the biological imperative, however, lead to modes of approaching phenomena that can only increase confusion and foster the pursuit of answers to pseudoproblems. In the next chapter we will present an orientation to the study of behavior and its development that minimizes these difficulties.

Chapter Three

The Beginnings
of a Resolution:
A Modern Synthesis

One problem that lies at the root of all four of the philosophical positions described in Chapter Two (hierarchy of science, reductionism, culture–biology dualism, the biological imperative) is the confusion between scientific activity and nature itself. It is good to remember that all products of scientific activity are symbolic abstractions from nature, based on categories that may be formed differently at different times and by different investigators. In other words, a multitude of different questions can be asked, and a multitude of different answers can be devised, about the same event. Whether or not a particular answer is acceptable will depend not on some absolute truth or falsity but primarily on whether it is addressed to the interests and aims of the questioner. For example, if you were to ask "Why did you write this book?" and we were to answer in terms of the neuromuscular apparatus that allows coordination between hand, eye, and brain, you would undoubtedly feel that your question had been avoided. On the other hand, an answer in terms of our purposes and intentions would be appropriate, even if not complete or accurate enough to be entirely satisfactory to everyone. There are, of course, further criteria by which an answer is judged, such as the completeness with which it accounts for the phenomenon and its consistency with other knowledge (see Kaplan, 1964).

As we stated earlier, disciplines are distinguishable from one another by virtue of the fact that they look at nature differently—that they have unique interests, aims, methods, and techniques. To a lesser degree any two individual scientists are also distinguishable in this way. Even a single scientist can hold to different interests and aims with different materials of study or at different times. This diversity provides the excitement of scientific investigation, but it also entails some dangers. The dangers become especially apparent when different disciplines become interested in the same or similar phenomena. Frequently, the questions posed by the different disciplines are not phrased clearly enough to allow one to know whether or not the answers provided are appropriate. Under these circumstances, arguments — sometimes very extended and divisive ones — may be waged over the correctness of what seem to be two alternative answers to the same question. If these two "answers" really belong to two quite distinct questions, then, clearly, the argument will not be resolved until the questions themselves are separated, examined, and clarified. As you might imagine, there have been many such misdirected arguments in the interface of biology and psychology. Perhaps the most dramatic and prevalent has been the prolonged argument over whether behavioral development is innately or environmentally determined.

The Concept of Innateness

Lehrman (1970) has argued that the innate-versus-acquired controversy reflects both a semantic confusion concerning the word *innate* and a conceptual confusion about the relative importance of different kinds of behavioral investigation.

The Semantic Confusion

The word *innate* has often been used in theorizing about human, and other animal, behavioral development. In this sense, it refers to notions of developmental *fixity*. That is, the organization of innate behavioral patterns is presumed to develop in the absence of any significant influence from the environment. Support for this idea is usually sought in genetic studies. However, when geneticists say that a behavior pattern is innate, they mean simply that they can make a prediction about the distribution of the pattern among members of an offspring population if given knowledge about the distribution of the behavior in the parent population and about who mates with whom. In the geneticists' use of the word, nothing is implied about the role of the environment during the development of the pattern or about the consequences of changing environmental circumstances for the distribution of the pattern in the offspring population.

The Conceptual Confusion

The conceptual confusion arises as a consequence of investigators' differing interests in behavior. If an investigator is interested mainly in how the behavior enables the organism to achieve something important for its survival, then previous developmental events will be perceived as *leading to* the occurrence of this behavior. Development of behavior will be viewed, from this perspective, as a predetermined event involving the influence of a very limited number of factors, usually not including environmental experiences of the organism. If, however, the investigator is interested primarily in ascertaining the ontogenetic causes of some behavior, then the behavior will be perceived as *arising from* the preceding developmental events, including environmental experiences.

Consider, for example, the observation that a newly hatched laughing-gull chick will approach and peck the parent's beak in response to the sound of the "croon-call" of the parent. The behavioral investigator interested in the consequences of behavior knows that, if the young gull chick does not respond appropriately to the croon-call of the parent, its chances of survival will be reduced. The parent uses this call to attract the chicks, so that they will approach and peck the parent's bill, thereby stimulating the regurgitation of the food on which the chicks feed. Because of the vital importance of this response to the croon-call, it might be argued that the young laughing-gull chick is *designed* with the ability to make the response. Indeed, even embryos apparently can discriminate the croon-call from other adult calls, two days before hatching!

Taking a more causal perspective, Impekoven and Gold (1973) have shown that the discrimination of the croon-call is developmentally dependent on this call's being heard by the chicks before they hatch. During incubation, the parent gull frequently makes croon-like calls while resettling on the eggs. Several days before hatching, the parent's croon-like calls tend to increase the activity of the embryo, and, later, they increase its peeping. The activity and peeping inside the egg in turn stimulate the parent to make more resettling movements and, hence, more croon-like calls. Chicks hatched in incubators do not show the typical responses to crooning but rather crouch or try to hide. Therefore, prehatching exposure to parental calls is a prerequisite for later filial responses vital for the survival of the young.

This example illustrates the importance of avoiding the conceptual confusion that can arise when investigators approach developmental phenomena with different interests. The causal perspective should not be seen as somehow lacking in respect for the important consequences of the behavior for the survival of the chick and, hence, the species or as suggesting that the function of behavior should not also be studied.

Keeping Questions Distinct

Because the precise specification of questions is such an important preliminary scientific process and can be very disruptive to scientific investigation if overlooked, we would like to distinguish some of the major categories of questions that have been asked about behavior. Tinbergen (1951, 1963) described four questions that he saw as distinct within biology as a whole and applied them to the study of behavior. These four questions can be grouped into two broad categories: questions of function and questions of causation. Functional questions require answers in terms of the effects of behavior. Causative questions require answers in terms of the antecedent conditions of the behavior. Because each of the four questions is distinct, an answer to any one of them will not be an answer to any of the others. As you shall see, this rather subtle point may sometimes not be grasped by even the best of investigators.

Functional Questions

Functions, or the effects of behavior, can often be observed in individuals behaving in the here and now. Soon after its eggs hatch, a black-headed gull will get up from its nest, pick up the broken eggshell in its beak, fly or walk some distance from its nest, and drop the shell. This behavior serves the function, for the individual gull, of getting the eggshell out of the nest. We usually acknowledge this functional aspect of behavior by describing the entire sequence of movement patterns in terms of action, or in terms of the end result; in this case, we speak of eggshell removal regardless of whether the gull walks, runs, flies, or hires a van.

Functional questions can be divided into two distinct types (Beer, 1973). Function in the sense of the end accomplished by an individual's act—*biological function*—does not mean the same thing as function in terms of contribution to the survival of the species—*survival value*. Biologists must describe—and manipulate—quite different things when answering these two types of functional questions—despite the fact that the terms *function* and *adaptation* may be used to designate the subject matter of interest in both types of investigation. To determine that the biological function of the black-headed gull's behavior toward its eggshells is eggshell removal, one has only to observe systematically the relationship between the behavior and the immediate end achieved by the behavior—that is, the removal of the eggshell from the nest. But, to determine the survival value of eggshell removal, Tinbergen and his associates had to investigate the relationships between the presence of eggshells, their removal, and reproductive success. They found that the presence of a broken eggshell, with its conspicuous white interior, helps predators locate otherwise camouflaged nests, or, to put it the other way around, eggshell removal makes it more difficult for predators to find black-headed-gull nests; hence, eggshell removal has survival value because it reduces predation (Tinbergen, 1965).

Careful investigations, both descriptive and experimental, of the survival value of behavior have occurred only within the zoological tradition leading to modern ethology. Such investigations require one to study groups and changes in groups. Psychologists, however, like physiologists, are interested in individuals. The phenomenon that so intrigued the early functionalists and behaviorists, clearly traceable to the influence of physiologists such as Loeb and Jennings, was the fact that behavior was regulatory—that it could change or be modified to fit the exigencies of an environment in flux. When psychologists use a term such as *function*, they usually have in mind biological function, or the end accomplished by individual action. Frequently, survival value is inferred from information about biological function by the reasoning that the animal would not so behave unless its behavior were relevant to its survival in the evolutionary sense. Although this inference may often be correct, it is not necessarily so. Rigorous empirical support is required before the survival value of a behavior pattern can be established. Unfortunately, failure to distinguish between these two kinds of functional questions prevails today and is particularly noticeable in many of the popular discussions of the role of ethology in the investigation of human behavioral development.

Because there are behavioral differences between men and women, because some precursors of these differences are often found in young children, because these differences result in somewhat different social experiences, and because these differences bear some similarity to differences observed in other animals, it is sometimes concluded that these behavioral differences are of value for the survival of the human species (Freedman, 1968; Tiger & Fox, 1971). But, even though sex-related behavioral differences may be of consequence for the individuals exhibiting them, one cannot simply assume that they are the result of natural selection.

Function as Separate from Causation

Perhaps even more damaging than the confusion of the two meanings of function is the confusion of causation with function. For example, the black-headed gull does not appreciate the fact that broken shells aid predators in finding their eggs and young. A gull may, on occasion, pick up an eggshell, fly about with it, and then drop it near its own or a neighbor's nest.

The early interest in the function of behavior for the individual led to the recognition that an animal, when prevented from achieving the usual goal or function of a behavior, will *change* that behavior in such a way that the original goal or function is achieved. Moreover, any behavior that results in a rapid and efficient attainment of that goal will be exhibited whenever the circumstances appropriate to that function are present. Thus, an animal will exhibit a change in behavior when that change results in the attainment of some needed commodity, such as food. Because behavior frequently has effects that make sense to the person observing the behavior, there have been many instances within psychology of researchers' looking to *function* for causative explanations. However, as we have pointed out, psychologists have not typically distinguished biological function from survival value. Therefore, it is not always clear whether the causes are thought to lie in the immediate consequences or in survival value. For example, because an animal may learn to perform a task in order to get food, it has been suggested that the animal has a hunger drive that impels the food-getting behavior.

The instinct theory once espoused by McDougall (1926/1973) is a clear example of the confusion of functional and causal questions, because it is explicitly teleological. According to this doctrine, an animal's behavior looks sensible and purposive because the ends of the acts are somehow "in" the organism from the outset. The behavior is *caused by* its purpose. Although McDougall's blatant teleology was attacked and discarded on the grounds that it was pseudoexplanatory, other, more subtle forms of the argument, such as drive theory, have survived.

Causal Questions

Tinbergen (1963) divides causative questions into three types— immediate, historical (phylogenetic), and ontogenetic—in part on the basis of the length of time taken into account.

Proximate causation. At the level of the individual and on a short time scale there is causation equivalent to what we usually mean when we speak of causes—*immediate, or proximate, causation.* The immediate causes of behavior are those antecedent events that contribute to the performance and organization of a behavior pattern. Some of these events are external and some internal to the organism. For example, the black-headed gull removes eggshells because they possess certain stimulative properties—a broken contour and contrasting interior—and because the gull is in a particular reproductive condition that is potentially describable in terms of hormone levels and nervous-system "state." The study of immediate causation is the familiar activity of most of psychology and physiology.

Phylogenetic causation. A second type of causative question covers a much longer time span. This is *historical, or phylogenetic, causation,* or causation that may be traced back over several generations. From the biologist's point of view, questions about phylogenetic causation are evolutionary questions: What were the phylogenetic precursors of this behavior? What was the original characteristic that was changed, over many generations and as a function of natural selection, into the present form? This line of questioning leads to questions concerning the nature of the "gene pool" of the population, the pressures for food and space provided by other populations, the changing conditions of the ecological system of which the population is a part, the effects of predators, changes in mating patterns, geological changes, and so on. Because behavior leaves few fossils, the phylogenetic question is one of the most difficult to answer. Many techniques for investigating the behavior of contemporary animals have been suggested as providing plausible answers to phylogenetic questions, but all of them exhibit severe conceptual weaknesses (Atz, 1970). Nevertheless, the plausible arguments that have been formed provide some intriguing notions about the evolution of behavior. For example, it is believed that many courtship and other communication patterns have evolved, through a process called *ritualization*, out of patterns more closely tied to individual survival. Thus, part of the courtship behavior of a male mallard duck consists of his pointing his bill, in a highly stereotyped fashion, at a conspicuous feather on his wing. Examination of the behavior patterns of mallards and other duck species suggest that this behavior evolved out of the phylogenetically older feather-cleaning behavior pattern.

 Ontogenetic causation.   The third type of causative question distinguished by Tinbergen concerns *ontogenetic, or developmental, causation.* The time span covered by this type of question is the lifetime of the individual. The search for ontogenetic causes may be thought of as simply a backward extension of the study of immediate causes, provided one remembers that there may be important differences between the way scientists think about events having immediate effects and the way they think about events having effects removed in time. Unlike historical causes, both immediate and developmental causes operate within the life span of an individual. A major source of confusion in the history of the developmental study of behavior, in both biology and psychology, has been the formation of categories of *developmental* causes based on *phylogenetic* questions about behavior. Lorenz (1965) distinguished between "phylogenetic" and "ontogenetic" sources of information but went on to assert that phylogenetic sources shape development through readout from the genetic blueprint, whereas ontogenetic sources have a modifying influence through the individual's learning from the physical and sociocultural environments. It is implied by this distinction that one could dichotomize different behavior patterns, or even a single behavior pattern, into a learned component and a genetic, or phylogenetic, component. Lorenz thus continues to confuse evolutionary questions with developmental causal ones. To understand the phylogenetic history of a behavior pattern or to understand its function in individual or species survival *is not* to understand the developmental causes that must operate if the behavior is to be expressed.

 Understanding the developmental cause of any behavior pattern involves investigating

> the development of new *structures* and activity *patterns* from the resolution of the interaction of *existing* structures and patterns, within the organism and its internal environment, and between the organism and its outer environment. At any stage of development, the new features emerge from the interactions within the *current* stage and between the *current* stage and the environment. The interaction out of which the organism develops is *not* one, as is so often said, between heredity and environment. It is between *or-*

ganism and environment! And the organism is different at each different stage of its development [Lehrman, 1953, p. 345].

Moreover, the environment may differ at different developmental stages of the organism.

The organism and its environment are in a reciprocal relationship. The environment shapes the organism and its behavior while the organism and its behavior are shaping the environment. The task of the developmental psychologist is to detail precisely the individual ontogenetic nature of this reciprocal relationship as it pertains to the occurrence of any particular behavior pattern. Carrying out this task involves having an understanding of the physiological and biochemical processes of the organism as they affect behavior, as well as knowing how the experiences of the environmental events and conditions encountered by the organism affect its physiology, biochemistry, and behavior.

A Holistic and Epigenetic Approach to Developmental and Comparative Psychology

The orientation to the study of development proposed by T. C. Schneirla (1966) and elaborated by others (Lehrman, 1953, 1962, 1970; Moltz, 1965; Rosenblatt, 1970) nicely complements Tinbergen's four questions; it will serve as the conceptual framework for this book because it avoids most of the problems we have described that plague the formation of a developmental-psychobiology discipline. It is a *holistic* theory in the sense that it stresses that the object of interest in behavioral investigation is *the entire living and active organism as it exists in its species-typical environment*. The organism has a unity, which is the phenomenon to be understood, even though it may often have to be divided into analytic categories (hormonal aspects, neural aspects, social aspects, and so on) if it is to be understood. In other words, analytic investigations must always be in the service of a synthesis—namely, the understanding of the organism as a whole. It is an *epigenetic* approach because it asserts that *organisms always*, insofar as they are alive, *interact with a stimulative environment;* consequently, development is the progressive change effected in an individual through a lifetime of these interactions. Finally, or rather primarily, it is a *comparative* approach. A fundamental objective of the approach is an understanding of the similarities *and differences* in the organization of behavior of all living species. Moreover, it is an assumption of the approach that behavioral organization is best understood through the study of development. Hence, the theory is psychobiological without implying a duality in the organism, is comparative without ignoring the important behavioral differences among species, and is developmental in focus.

Schneirla's Perspective on Development

Development is conceived of by Schneirla as the progressive change in an organism from its beginning to its death; progressive change comes about as a result of an interaction between the *organism* and its *environment*. An animal's environment is sometimes spoken of as a *milieu* or *context*, perhaps as a reminder that environments must be defined from the point of view of the organism's capabilities. The same physical energies may have an effect on one organism but not another, or on an organism at one point in development but not at a different point.[1] Von Uexkull (1957) spoke of this personal quality of environments as the *Umwelt*, or perceptual/reactive world, of the organism. Appreciation of the Umwelt notion is important for an understanding of the differing effects of the same environmental conditions on development.

When we speak of an organism, we are speaking of a creature that has a past; it has already been through a series of interactions with its environment, and it is interacting with its environment while we talk about it or look at it. Schneirla argues that one may separate an organism from its environment for analytic purposes but that, in fact, for the organism they are inseparably fused. There can be no organism without an environmental context; such an eventuality is, quite simply, impossible.

From this perspective it is even possible to consider seriously the developmental consequences of *self-stimulation*. For example, young mallard ducklings approach and follow their mother primarily when she utters a special "assembly call." The behavior of the ducklings is not dependent on prior exposure to this maternal call; incubator-hatched ducklings will also approach the source of this call. Indeed, even the duck embryo shows signs of being responsive to this call.

In a series of ingenious experiments, Gottlieb (1971) was able to demonstrate that the duckling's responsiveness is dependent on prior exposure to either the prehatching peeps of its nestmates or *its own peeping!* These birds typically begin to vocalize some three to four days before hatching. When deprived of the sound of their own peeping and that of their siblings during the four days before hatching, they show no selective approach to the maternal assembly call after hatching. Interestingly, although the complete maternal call does not sound at all like the peeping the embryo makes before hatching, Gottlieb found that the part of the call to which the duckling is initially responsive is similar to the prehatching peep. Thus, the duckling's self-produced stimulation has an important influence on the development of social behaviors vital for its survival.

---

[1]Remember, an organism's activities also contribute to the construction of its environment, which in turn contributes to the developmental changes of the organism.

The Fusion of Maturation and Experience

A distinction between maturation and experience is frequently made in theories of development, but this distinction has a special meaning for the epigeneticist. *Maturation* refers to the processes of growth and differentiation. *Growth* is additive accumulation—of cells or of vocabulary words, for instance. *Differentiation* is the process by which the growing organism forms qualitatively different and specialized parts and processes—eyes, legs, nest-building abilities, language, concepts, and so on. Finally, *experience* is the effect of an organism's environment, or milieu, on these maturational processes.

Consider the organization of hatching behavior in bob-white quail. Although the eight or so eggs typically laid by a bob-white hen are laid one at a time at 24-hour intervals, all of the eggs hatch within an hour's time. That is, although there is an eight-day spread from the laying of the first egg to the laying of the last egg, there is only an hour from the hatching of the first egg to the hatching of the last. Vince (1974) showed that synchronized hatching (which is vital if the young are to survive) results from the embryos' stimulating each other before hatching. The loud clicking associated with embryonic respiration appears to be partly responsible for the synchronization, and, because the eggs must be in contact with one another for synchronization to occur, it can be assumed that the effective stimulus probably involves vibrations transmitted from one egg to another.

As a result of inter-egg social stimulation, developmentally advanced embryos are held back and hatch later than they would if kept in isolation. Moreover, this stimulation advances the hatching time of developmentally younger embryos. Because hatching requires not only postural and behavioral changes in the embryo but also metabolic, anatomical, and physiological changes appropriate for post-hatching existence, this elegant study is an excellent illustration of the fusion of maturation and experience in normal development.

The Concept of Experience

The epigenetic view of the sort of event that can provide an experience for an organism is very broad. It is not possible to define all possible categories of experience a priori; this is an empirical question that must be investigated for each organism and for each developmental process in which one is interested. It follows, therefore, that experience is not synonymous with learning through conditioning, practice, or observation. Learning as it is customarily defined is but one aspect of experience; whether or not it is an important aspect for the development of a specific behavior pattern is an interesting and important question but not the *only* interesting and important *experiential* question that may need to be asked about the development of the pattern. For example, male guinea pigs that have been raised in isolation from other guinea pigs respond to receptive females when they become adult with less sexual behavior than normally reared males (Valenstein, Riss, & Young, 1955). If they are reared in individual wire-mesh cages so that they can smell and see other guinea pigs but have no contact with them, their sexual behavior as adults will be equivalent to that of normal guinea pigs (Gerall, 1963). In this instance, experience with social stimuli during development, even when these stimuli are totally divorced from any sexual behavior, will influence adult sexual behavior. The developmental organization of guinea-pig sexual behavior is not fully understood, but clearly experience can have an influence unpredictable from any of the conventional theories of learning.

Although it is helpful to distinguish maturation from experience, this should by no means be construed as suggesting that there are two separate processes in the organism—one dependent on the environment and one not. Both growth and differentiation depend on the environment in a very involved and crucial way. There is evidence that this dependency is characteristic of anatomical as well as behavioral aspects of organisms.

Many anatomical organizations are complex enough actually to allow for their reorganization by function. For instance, the cat's visual system is a very complex anatomical structure. Within the retina of the eye, there are several kinds of neural cells, including those that are stimulated to discharge by light (receptor cells), those that discharge when stimulated by certain temporal and spatial patterns of receptor-cell discharges (bipolar cells), and those that discharge when stimulated by certain temporal and spatial patterns of stimulation by bipolar cells (ganglion cells). The information contained in the light reaching the eye is both detected and transformed by the anatomical organization of the neural connections in the retina even before reaching the brain. In addition, the retina contains two other kinds of cells (amacrine and horizontal), which seem to affect the sensitivity of bipolar and ganglion cells. Interestingly, there is some evidence that these horizontal and amacrine cells receive stimulation from neurons located in the brain. As you shall see, these centrifugal connections (as they are called) can be an important anatomical prerequisite for functional reorganization of the visual system.

Projecting from the retina, nerve fibers from the ganglion cells make connections with both the superior colliculus (or old visual system) and the lateral geniculate of the brain. Nerve fibers from the lateral geniculate make connections with the cells of area 17 of the cerebral cortex. These cells, in turn, connect with cells in visual-association areas 18 and 19 of the cortex, which contribute fibers to the myriad connection system of the so-called association areas of the cerebral cortex. Visual information from the superior colliculus is also transmitted to the cerebral cortex via connections with the thalamus. The neuroanatomical connections in the cat's visual system—particularly those between the retina and the brain—are highly specific. If the nerve fibers connecting the retina to the lateral geniculate are cut, each fiber

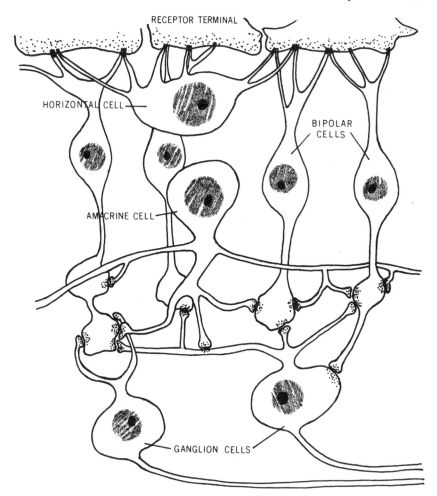

Figure 3–1. The axons of the ganglion cells in the retina of the eye form the optic nerve, which neurologically connects the eye to the brain. Thus, the information carried by the optic nerve from the retina to the brain is not simply a reproduction of the pattern of light falling on the retina. Rather, information is "constructed" for the brain by the pattern of connections and activity among the other neural cells that connect the ganglion cells to the light-receptor cells. Adapted from "Synaptic Organization of the Frog Retina: An Electron Microscopic Analysis Comparing the Retinas of Frogs and Primates," *Proceedings of the Royal Society of London,* 1968, *170,* 205–228. Used by permission.

will grow back and reestablish the connection with the exact lateral-geniculate cell from which it was severed.

Electrophysiological recording from individual cells within the visual system shows that the anatomical connections lead to some specific patterns of

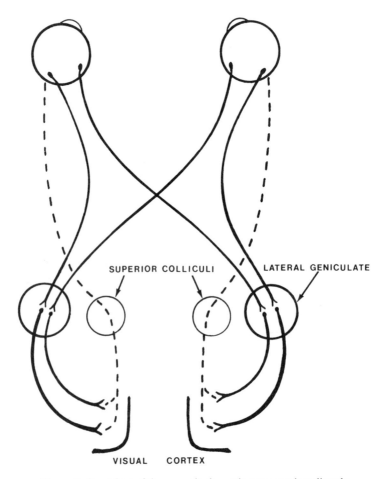

Figure 3–2.   Most of the axons in the optic nerve project directly
to the left and right lateral geniculate bodies in the brain. There
they connect with cells that project axons to area 17 of the cortex
(the visual cortex). However, a small portion of axons in the optic
nerve do not project to the lateral geniculate bodies but rather make
connections with cells in the left and right superior colliculi. The
cells in the superior colliculi project axons to many different parts
of the brain, including the visual cortex.

neural sensitivity to external stimulation. For example, Hubel and Wiesel
(1962) found that each cell in area 17 of the visual cortex responds maximally
to a line of light projected onto the retina. Moreover, each cell responds best
to a different specific orientation of the line. That is, some cells were found
that respond to lines oriented horizontally, some that respond to lines oriented
vertically, and others that respond to each angle in between. In a normal cat,
there is about the same number of cells in area 17 that respond preferentially to

each angle of orientation of a line of light. The cells in areas 18 and 19 are responsive to even more complex organizations of stimulation, such as angles and breaks in the contour of a line. From this it can be concluded that the neural cells of the cat's visual cortex detect specific features of stimulation as a consequence of their anatomical connections.

The notion of feature-detecting cells has had a major influence on the study of perceptual development. Some investigators have assumed that, as a consequence of the prenatal anatomical development of the visual system, the human infant is born with a set of feature detectors that becomes organized into more and more complex perceptual abilities during postnatal development (Hershenson, 1971). Indeed, the human infant's visual activities during the three to six months after birth are best described as the detection of a small number of specific features, such as lines and angles.

In a rather important study of visually naïve kittens, Barlow and Pettigrew (1971) found that, although many area-17 cells responded to line stimuli, not a single cell showed any orientation preference. That is, each cell responded to lines of any orientation. How, then, do cells acquire their orientation specificity? Blakemore and Cooper (1970; Blakemore, 1973, 1974) showed that visual experience with oriented lines can construct the orientation specificity of individual cells. They reared kittens, for several hours each day, in a circular enclosure painted with either horizontal or vertical stripes. The kittens wore special collars to prevent visual experience with their own bodies and were kept in the dark when not in the striped arena. Electrophysiological recording of the cells of area 17 showed that they responded only to horizontally oriented lines if the kitten had been reared in a horizontally striped world and only to vertically oriented lines if the kitten had been reared in a vertically striped world. In addition, the behavior of the kittens indicated that they were blind to line stimuli oriented at angles the opposite of those encountered in their rearing environment. Thus, the functioning of the visual system, as affected by the visual world, had significantly altered the system's fine structural organization. Indeed, given the complexity of the cat's visual system, such an organizing effect is not surprising.

Recent electrophysiological evidence has shown that the feature-detecting ability of many neurons of the visual cortex is altered by the typical activity of the cat. For example, horizontal-line detectors become vertical-line detectors when the cat is tilted 90° to one side (Horn, Stechler, & Hill, 1972). Apparently, the muscular and vestibular stimulation provided by the tilt changes the pattern of retinal ganglion cells affecting the visual cortex. Moreover, because of the centrifugal fibers entering the retina, the feature-detecting abilities of the retinal ganglion cells can be altered by activation of various parts of the central nervous system (Spinelli & Pribram, 1967). Thus, because of the complexity of the neuroanatomical structure of the visual system and because of the connections of the structure with other parts of the nervous system, visual perception is not the consequence just of light stimulation and of the way in which the neurons of the retina are connected to the brain. The environment is not only a good provider, giving sustenance for growth, as the predeterminists would have us believe; it is also a source of structure for the developing organism. There are trace effects of experience woven into all aspects of the developing organism. In other words, the organism does not unfold from some preformed blueprint but rather derives its organization, as it progressively changes, from what it is at present and from the stimulative context within which it behaves. What an organism is like at point X + Y in time will depend on what it was like at point X and what its experiences were like during the period of transition from X to X + Y. It is possible, from this viewpoint, to envision a multiplicity of alternative developmental outcomes and to see that one outcome might be reachable by different pathways. This view is to be contrasted with the one that asserts that there is one path and one outcome, dictated by an unfolding of previously encoded instructions; from this latter perspective, any deviation from "proper outcome" would have to be viewed as an abnormality brought about by an unsupportive environment. Interestingly, by discarding the notion of a determined and fixed developmental end, an epigeneticist is led to the position that abnormality, if it is to have a meaning, must be defined by criteria other than deviation from a proper outcome.

The Relationship between Evolution and Development

Phyletic levels. Before one can understand how Schneirla conceives of the relationship between evolution and development, one must have a firm idea of his concept of *phyletic levels.* Schneirla repeatedly asserts that we ought not to take our concepts or methods fully formed from other disciplines. If psychologists are interested in ordering the relations among various species, they must set themselves a task of behavioral analysis of all living forms and base their ordering on their analyses. Because psychologists have only *living* species to work with, their ordering cannot turn out to be a reconstruction of the temporal order of evolution (the phylogenetic tree of systematists). Schneirla suggests that we begin to understand the differences among species by noting gross differences in behavioral complexity. Species that operate at a similar level of behavioral complexity would thus be said to occupy the same phyletic level. An ordering of phyletic levels is very similar to an ordering based on major evolutionary changes that have presumably occurred over geologic time. There are exceptions, however. Evolutionarily more advanced creatures may occupy a lower phyletic level as determined by analyses of their behavioral complexity (Maier & Schneirla, 1935; Schneirla, 1949, 1962).

The difference separating phyletic levels is a difference in complexity, or behavioral plasticity, and one way to characterize the complexity of behavior is in terms of the relationship between structures and function, or between the apparatus with which one behaves and behavior itself. For example, there is a highly limited number of things that an insect can possibly do with its appendages. But, because of the structure of human appendages, people can do a larger variety of things with theirs. It is thus important to study the role that structure plays in behavior. The more freedom there is between structure and function, the more complex the behavioral organization. If a structure can be used in only one or two ways, then we may have understood the development of the behavior associated with the structure simply by understanding the development of that structure.

The notion of phyletic levels as related to the structure–function relationship is particularly important to bear in mind when making analogies between the behaviors of different organisms. For instance, some linguists have likened the innate knowledge of linguistic rules that is presumed to be a part of the human nervous system to the innate knowledge of the physical rules of web construction possessed by the spider's nervous system. Nobody teaches the spider how to build a web, nor does anyone instruct the child in the basic rules of language. As with the child, the spider seems to know the rules simply by being a normal spider with a normal nervous system. A linguist might argue that, if we can accept the spider's knowledge of web construction as innate, we should also be able to accept the child's knowledge of basic linguistic rules as innate.

Examined from the perspective of phyletic levels, the analogy is superficial, faulty, and of no use for the understanding of language development. The spider is a land invertebrate, having no internal skeleton of bones and requiring, therefore, an exoskeleton of hardened waxy chiton for support and locomotion. There is a sharp physical limit to the mass an animal can achieve if it possesses an exoskeleton. This limit in mass obviously limits the number of cells of the animal and consequently the number of cells devoted to each tissue, organ, and system of the animal. Because of these limitations, one invertebrate neuron does the work of many vertebrate neurons in the control of muscular movements. The vertebrate nervous system, therefore, can achieve a greater refinement of muscular movement and has more plasticity of movement than the invertebrate system (Vowles, 1961). Moreover, the neurons of the invertebrate central nervous system are much fewer in number, are more highly specific and delimited in their connections with other neurons, and are relatively refractory to the consequences of experience by comparison with vertebrate central nervous system neurons (Cohen, 1970). In other words, the structure of the spider's nervous system is organized with fewer alternative pathways and fewer opportunities for interconnections among pathways than is the nervous system of human beings. This results in a greater correspondence, for the theorist, between knowledge of neural structure and the explanation of the behavior for the spider than for the human.

Interestingly, Witt, Reed, and Peakall (1969) have demonstrated that part of the "knowledge of physical rules" necessary for web construction resides in the length and number of joints of the spider's legs and the physical characteristics of the environment in which the web is spun. Saying that the spider spins webs according to some innate knowledge does not indicate the means by which spiders achieve web construction. Whatever the means used to accomplish some behavior of an animal, whether it be web construction or language construction, the notion of phyletic levels cautions against inferring that those same means are responsible for the accomplishment of similar behaviors of other animals.

Functional order. Schneirla uses the concept of *functional order* to communicate the fact that there are behaviors of different complexity *within* each phyletic level. "The highest functional orders characterizing any psychological level are those utilizing its maximal possible gains through ontogeny" (Schneirla, 1957, p. 85). Random escape from a frightening stimulus is a behavior with a low functional order; the coordinated hunting pattern of a carnivore or the orderly movements to food, water, and shelter of the leaders of a monkey troop are behaviors with a high functional order. A longer ontogeny will allow an animal to add more behavior of higher functional orders to its repertoire of low-order behavior. Clearly, the human species is more complex than others in the sense of having a larger repertoire of behaviors with a high functional order.

It is necessary to study the ontogeny of each species in which one is interested, because species may differ not only in their adult forms but throughout their ontogeny. It is impossible to extrapolate directly from one species to another, because a capacity that develops in a particular way in one species may develop in quite another way in a second species. Both precocial birds, such as chicks and ducklings, and human babies learn the perceptual attributes of their parents (voice qualities, color and shape characteristics, and so on), but the rapid learning process in precocial birds bears only a superficial resemblance to the human learning process. Ants and rats are both good at finding their way about in mazes, but the processes through which they accomplish this task differ markedly (Schneirla, 1957).

Natural selection has operated on behavioral capacities throughout ontogeny, but the processes of natural selection are opportunistic; they will make use of whatever the organism already has. The fact that a behavioral capacity has an evolutionary function tells us nothing about its development, and the fact that many behaviors share the designation *species-typical*[2] does not mean that they have all developed in the same manner. Each species and each behavior pattern must be studied separately before statements can be made about the course of their development.

---

[2]Behaviors that are typically exhibited by all members of a species and not usually exhibited by members of other species.

The Relationship between the Organism and Its Behavior

The concept of levels is important to an understanding of the development of the individual and to an understanding of the role of behavior in that individual's development (Birch, 1971). Any organism can be characterized as consisting of many levels of organization, or systems, ranging from those characteristic of single cells to those involving the relationship of the whole organism to its environment. The simpler systems at each level become important components of the higher-level systems. Each system has emergent properties unique to its level of organization as well as having the properties of its lower-level components. Furthermore, these emergent properties have a causal capacity. That is, they can produce effects, or changes. For example, the water molecule H_2O has emergent properties that are unique to it as well as the properties characteristic of the hydrogen (H) and oxygen (O) atoms. Of course, knowledge of the properties of hydrogen and oxygen atoms is important for an understanding of the properties of H_2O, but this knowledge alone will not allow the prediction of all the properties of water. Moreover, many of the emergent properties of water can have a causal effect on the individual properties of hydrogen and oxygen (emphasizing some properties, inhibiting others) in addition to their effect on other molecules and systems of which water is a component.

Roger Sperry (1965) provides a very clear presentation of this notion of levels as related to brain functioning.

At the lower-most levels . . . we have local aggregates . . . of subnuclear particles interacting with great energy, all within the neutrons and protons of their respective atomic nuclei. These chaps, of course, do not have very much to say about what goes on in the affairs of the brain, . . . because they are all firmly trapped . . . by their atomic [nuclei, which] . . . are . . . firmly controlled in turn. The various atomic elements are "molecule-bound"—that is, they are hauled and pushed around by the larger spatial and configurational forces of their encompassing molecules.

Similarly, the molecules of the brain are . . . pretty well bound up . . . by their respective cells and tissues . . . . The brain molecules are obliged to submit to a course of activity in time and space that is largely determined . . . by the over-all dynamic and spatial properties of the whole cell . . . . Even brain cells . . . do not have very much to say about when they are going to fire their messages . . . or in what time pattern they will fire them . . . . The flow and timing of [neural activity is] . . . governed largely by . . . properties of the whole cerebral circuit, within which the given cells and fibers are incorporated, and also by the relationship of this circuit system to other circuit systems. Further, . . . the general circuit properties of the whole brain may undergo radical and widespread changes [as a result of] . . . cerebral "set"— . . . a shifting pattern of central excitation . . . [opening or priming] . . . one group of circuit pathways [having special properties] . . . while . . . closing, repressing, or inhibiting . . . other circuit potentialities . . . . Of course, all of the simpler . . . electric, atomic, molecular, cellular and physiological forces remain present . . . and . . . continue to operate, . . . but these lower level forces and properties have been superceded . . . by those [of higher levels of organization], . . . [and] proper function in the uppermost levels always depends on normal operation at subsidiary levels [p. 79].[3]

When one adds to Sperry's description of causal relations the organization of the individual as a whole and the individual's functioning within an organized social and physical milieu, the sources for the organization of behavior can be seen to be quite extensive. The emergence of organized patterns of behavior involves the coordinated action of sensory, neuromuscular, skeletal/muscular, hormonal, and central nervous systems, which, in part, depends on specifics of the social and physical milieu. The behavior, in turn, contributes to the condition or state of every one of these subsystems of the individual via the sensory, or experiential, feedback provided by both its *performance* and the *consequences* of its performance on the world.

This means that, although behavior is dependent on certain lower-level physiological events, it is also a contributing cause of such physiological events. A primary task of the developmental investigator is to define and clarify the nature of these reciprocal causal relationships as they exist among the different levels of organization within the organism. Used in this way, an epigenetic approach can be psychobiological without being reductionistic and without implying a duality in the organism. An epigenetic approach can, therefore, serve as a useful conceptual framework not only for the integration of biological disiciplines into developmental psychology but also for the investigation and resolution of many specifically human developmental problems.

By now, you may well be wondering what all of these examples about laughing gulls, ducklings, and cats have to do with human development. The developmental concepts and notions outlined in this chapter are not foreign to researchers and theorists interested in human development. However, because of the necessary limitations on human experimental research, human evidence in support of these notions can never be incontrovertibly presented.

Summary

We have attempted, in this chapter, to present a conceptual framework that permits the avoidance of many of the problems facing an integration of the psychological and biological perspectives. The conceptual framework is designed to keep developmental questions distinct from functional and phylogenetic questions. Preserving this distinction will not only help developmental psychologists avoid pseudoanswers but also obligates them to pursue developmental investigations of developmental questions.

In order to fully appreciate the important distinctions between developmental and evolutionary pursuits, one needs to be able to share the perspective of evolutionists. The next chapter will present this perspective.

Chapter Four

Genetics, Evolution, and Development

Conventional wisdom has it that every person is born with a set of intellectual and personal capabilities that is unlike anyone else's. The development of these capabilities is also unique to each individual, as a result of the variations in opportunity provided by society. Consequently, inequalities of accomplishment in any human endeavor reflect the combination of genetic and societal differences among people. Which of these two sources of inequality is more important is believed to be one of the most important issues facing a democratic society. It is possible that a major reorganization of the social, political, and educational structures of society will be the result of the resolution of this issue. Therefore, the issue is not simply academic.

Most psychology textbooks reflect the conventional wisdom in the way in which they incorporate discussions of genetics into chapters about personality, intelligence, and development. In the prevailing view, the role of genetics in psychological investigation is like the role of clay in sculpture. An individual's genetic makeup (genotype) is the clay out of which the environment, particularly through learning processes, sculpts all the substantial and interesting facets of psychological development. And, just as the characteristics of clay limit the free expression of the sculptor, so, too, do the characteristics of the individual's genotype limit the impact of the environment.

Of late, there has been a new interest in this presumed *limiting* characteristic of individual genotype. The modern techniques of the psychometricians and quantitative geneticists have been hailed as the means by which the relative importance of genetic and societal sources of inequalities among both individuals and groups of individuals may finally be ascertained. Much of the current interest in genetics was prompted by Arthur Jensen's (1969) review of the data on intelligence testing, the effectiveness of compensatory education, and the inheritance of intelligence. Jensen concluded that intelligence is highly heritable and that children who score low on intelligence tests lack the capacity for abstract reasoning. Moreover, he asserted that any differences between Black and White children in IQ scores may well reflect genetic differences between the groups. Jensen's conclusions, if you remember, aroused a good deal of interest among social scientists, educators, and public officials.

We suspect that Jensen's review merely precipitated the expression of a general dissatisfaction with the techniques, expense, and effectiveness of the various "compensatory-" and special-education programs initiated and supported by the government during the 1960s. Interestingly, all societal reform movements based on traditional psychological theory and methods—from the rehabilitation of criminals to new strategies in the education of typical and atypical children—have recently come under heavy attack. The identification of a genetic origin for any of the behavior problems currently capturing the public's attention (such as criminal aggression, sex offenses, schizophrenia, and mental retardation) is seized upon by a dissatisfied public and used as an argument either for a return to traditional methods of dealing with these problems—namely, punishment and/or isolation of "affected" individuals—or for the use of newer, so-called biological, methods requiring alterations of an individual's chemical milieu (chemotherapy) or anatomical organization (psychosurgery—including neural and gonadal removal).

It may be the commitment to one or another of the different methods of dealing with behavior problems rather than an understanding of genetics that has contributed to the emergence of two popular positions regarding the role of genetics in human development. Opinion seems to be divided between the view that there is no possibility of any significant relationship between psychology and genetics and the view that genes determine most, if not all, of the currently most interesting psychological characteristics (intelligence, aggression, and so on). Both positions, when carefully examined, exhibit rather fundamental misconceptions about the discipline of genetics. The conventional wisdom itself is also a misrepresentation of modern genetics. Therefore, a knowledge of modern genetics is necessary for anyone who wishes to avoid the conceptual pitfalls of the conventional wisdom.

The Nature of Genetics

There are really two kinds of geneticists. The population geneticist's ultimate concern is with questions about the evolution and formation of new species via natural selection or selective breeding. Using the simple technique of documenting or controlling who breeds with whom, this geneticist investigates the nature of a gene and its relationship to other genes and to the occurrence of physical and behavioral characters (phenotype). The second kind of geneticist—the molecular geneticist—is ultimately concerned with the role of DNA in the organization of cellular activity and the relationship between DNA characteristics and the characteristics of the gene as defined by the population geneticist. The relationship between these two kinds of genetics is far from being agreed upon and is the subject of a good deal of philosophical (Ayala & Dobzhansky, 1974; Hull, 1972) and theoretical (Crick, 1966; Mayr, 1969) debate. Before examining the relationship of genetics to developmental psychology, therefore, we would like to sketch briefly the historical antecedents of modern genetics.

The Origin of the Field of Genetics

Both genetics and developmental psychology have had relatively short histories as independent disciplines. It was with the rediscovery of Gregor Mendel's work at the turn of this century and the subsequent elaboration of the laws of inheritance and of the techniques for their investigation that genetics was established as an important discipline in biology. The laws and techniques of genetics so captivated the thought of biologists during the period from 1900 to 1930 that genetics was believed to preclude the need for Darwin's theory of evolution through natural selection as the explanation for the diversity of plants and animals. It was mainly through the efforts of a small group of biologists in the 1930s and 1940s that the discipline of genetics was finally wedded to Darwin's theory to form a "modern synthesis." This synthetic theory ("modern theory," "neo-Darwinian theory," "the synthetic theory") of evolution subsequently became the major theoretical framework for the whole of biological investigation (see Handler, 1970).

Darwin and the origin of species. Both Mendel and Darwin sought to account for variation and change. This is a most significant aspect of the thinking of both men because the earlier, predominant mode of thinking in biology was *typological* (Mayr, 1963). Typologists approach variation by asserting that only those aspects or characters that individuals have in common (the "essence" of individuals) are relevant for biology; individual differences are mere shadows on the wall. Before Darwin, it was commonly believed by the scientific community that each different species of plant and animal was separately and instantaneously created (by God) and that each represented the best design for living within its environment.[1] This notion is called *the fixity of species.* All species, with human beings excepted, were thought to be "in harmony with nature." So dominant was the idea of separate and instantaneous creation that, when the accumulation of fossil evidence indicated that many species that existed in the past do not exist in the present,

---

[1]The fields of anatomy and taxonomy were the most prestigious and popular areas of scientific investigation at the time. Both involved static structures and thus offered their researchers little incentive to think in terms of notions such as process, evolution, and development. One of Darwin's most significant contributions to biology was to reorient it away from static and toward dynamic concepts and ideas. Even the fields of anatomy and taxonomy took on a more dynamic flavor as a result, and the way was cleared for the ascendency of developmental biology, physiology, evolution, genetics, and ecology within the biological discipline.

it was postulated by many of the most prestigious scientists that the earth's history has consisted of a series of geological and biological catastrophes. Like the biblical flood, each catastrophe wiped out all or most of the life on earth, after which a new set of species was created, with some replacements, some additions, and some omissions. Thus, species were considered to be immutable and unrelated to one another. Moreover, the individual members of a species could not vary very much, else the harmony of life would be disrupted. Observable differences among individuals of the same species were considered to be artifacts of their peculiar life histories or the effects of their mode of capture or of the methods used in preserving specimens.

In the early 1800s, the theory of worldwide catastrophes received a major setback; the geologist Sir Charles Lyell compiled a great deal of evidence supporting the notion (previously espoused by Hutton) that the earth had not experienced any worldwide geological catastrophes but rather had undergone continuous and gradual transformation. Furthermore, he declared that the forces of change responsible for the history of geological change were *still operating*.

When Lyell's book first appeared, Darwin was studying for the clergy at Cambridge University. It was here that he met and befriended the professor of botany and orthodox Anglican minister J. S. Henslow. As a result of this friendship, Henslow recommended Darwin for a position aboard the H.M.S. *Beagle,* which was to sail on a five-year voyage, exploring the coast of South America. While on the voyage, Darwin described and collected samples of plants, animals, fossils, and rocks from the different places visited by the ship. Henslow had recommended Lyell's *Principles of Geology* as a guide for Darwin's geological investigations but had cautioned Darwin not to believe what it contained.

Henslow's selection was most fortunate; Lyell's book taught Darwin not only how to think about geology but how to think in general. "From him [Lyell], Charles learned observation in the highest sense of a thoughtful activity which suggests and tests hypotheses, . . . he learned how to construct hypotheses, . . . [and] he came to see nature as logical, regular, and self-explanatory" (Irvine, 1956, p. 37). Because geology was the most historical of sciences, many of the ingredients of the theory of evolution by natural selection were to be found in Lyell's book. Moreover, every place that Darwin went ashore along the South American coast was an incontrovertible demonstration of the validity of Lyell's theory of geology. Although all the data gathered during this trip together led to the development of the theory of evolution, one group of islands (the Galapagos) was particularly influential.

The Galapagos Archipelago is a series of volcanic islands in the eastern Pacific, far off the coast of South America. At no time have they ever been attached to the main continent; therefore, any species of plant or animal observed by Darwin on the islands had to have traveled over 600 miles of ocean to get there from South America. Darwin found some 13 species of finch (Geospiza) on the island, reminiscent of finches on the American main-land and having an underlying similarity to one another yet strikingly different from one another in both morphology and behavior. Could it be that a few pairs of finches from South America had been blown to the islands and, over the course of several generations, *changed* into the 13 separate species—having the bills, food preferences, eating habits, and other characteristics of birds other than finches? Indeed, this question could be asked of all the plants and animals appearing on the Galapagos Islands.

Because many of the ideas making up Darwin's theory of evolution are so apparently simple and readily understood, it is sometimes a surprise to the student that they had to wait so long for acceptance. Indeed, many of Darwin's contemporaries ridiculed him for only restating what many others, including some ancient Greek philosophers, had said. However, these critics mistakenly confused the philosophical notion of the chain of life with Darwin's evolutionary theory—a confusion, we might add, that is still preva-lent in the fields of both psychology (Hodos & Campbell, 1969) and biology (Nelson, 1970). Previous evolutionists had sought to arrange all the living species along a single line, which meant that the nonextinct species of birds had evolved from one of the nonextinct species of reptiles. Human beings were believed to have evolved from the chimpanzee.

Darwin's contribution was to show that all living species are related via descent from a common ancestor. Human and chimp are evolutionarily related not because humans evolved from chimps but because the two evolved separately from a now-extinct common ancestor. The evolutionary relation-ships among living species could best be represented, according to Darwinian ideas, by a tree, with the tips of the branches representing the living species and the connections of the branches with one another, and eventually with the main trunk, representing the descent from common ancestors. In this model, no living species can be considered better than any other living species, because they all represent the currently most successful point of their particu-lar branch. Moreover, Darwin's theory brought meaning and organization to a host of previously unrelated facts from the fields of embryology, taxonomy, physiology, and other biological disciplines. In the broadness of its scope, the theory of evolution has to rank as one of the greatest achievements of human intellect. It is no wonder, then, that many decades of scientific development (Irvine, 1956) and many years of cognitive growth (Gruber, 1966; Gruber & Barrett, 1974) had to take place before Darwin arrived at a satisfactory presen-tation of his theory.

Darwin's and Wallace's theory of evolution.   The theory of evolu-tion by natural selection was presented independently by two men—Charles Darwin and Alfred Russel Wallace. Examination of the similarities and differ-ences in their backgrounds is instructive regarding why they should happen to generate the same theory (Bronowski, 1973). Both men were products of the

British Victorian cultural milieu, which emphasized physical and intellectual exploration, long hours of work, and the careful, planned, and systematic use even of leisure time. However, Darwin was from a wealthy and somewhat famous family, whereas Wallace, who left school at 14 and went on to become a land surveyor, was from a poor, working-class family. Unlike Darwin, Wallace spent much of his lifetime earning a living.

Both men were ardent naturalists, attracted and awed by the vast diversity, complexity, and beauty of plants and animals. An interest in natural history was common in people in Darwin's social position; Wallace's interest, on the other hand, was apparently generated by his work—surveying the English countryside for railway robber barons. At the age of 25, Wallace decided to support himself by collecting foreign specimens and selling them to collectors and museums in England.

Both men visited South America and were dazzled by the diversity of plant and animal species and struck by the differences between neighboring species. Both began to wonder how neighboring species had become different. In a series of unlucky events, Wallace lost all of his specimens during the return trip to England. Nevertheless, he had become convinced, as had Darwin, by South America's wildlife that related species had diverged from a common stock.

Both men had read Malthus's *Essay on Population* and had realized that, if populations grow faster than their food supplies, then animals must compete to survive. Thus, nature acts, through differential survival, as a selective force, forming species to fit their environments. However, Darwin had arrived at the notion of evolution through natural selection much earlier than had Wallace, had discussed it with certain of his friends, and had written a small piece on it that he wanted his wife to have published after his death.

Finally, the two men had corresponded with each other and with many of the other well-known naturalists of the time. It is likely that Darwin's ideas and notions, as written to Wallace and other naturalists with whom Wallace corresponded, subtly influenced Wallace's thinking about evolution. Of course, it can never be known whether Wallace's ideas were stimulated by his casual knowledge of Darwin's work, but it is known that Wallace was ill with fever in February of 1858 on one of the islands in the Malay Archipelago when he remembered Malthus's book and realized that it could explain why species differ. He quickly wrote a paper on the subject and sent it to Darwin to show to Lyell, should he consider it worthwhile.

Darwin's friends prevailed on him to write a paper on the subject and saw to it that the two papers were simultaneously presented to the Linnean Society (a distinguished society of biologists and naturalists) of London in July of 1858. The papers caused not a stir. Darwin immediately wrote *The Origin of Species*—an outline of his theory—and changed the course of biology. Although Wallace continued to make substantial contributions to biology and to the theory of evolution after the appearance of Darwin's book, he never became fully integrated into the somewhat class-conscious society of British naturalists.

Darwin's theory, as outlined in *The Origin of Species*, had five main points.

1. The number of offspring produced always exceeds the number of parents. However, the total number of individuals in a species tends to remain more or less stable from one generation to the next.

2. There is variation among members of a species.

3. Given the conditions of the environment, certain variants will be more likely to survive than others. (This is the notion of natural selection.)

4. Offspring tend to inherit the characteristics of their parents; consequently, there is preservation of those characters that "fit" the conditions of the environment.

5. As the conditions of the environment changed during the history of the earth, species changed to fit the new circumstances. Therefore, all living species can be traced via a series of common ancestors back to the origin of life.

Darwin's later writings provided more empirical and theoretical support for the continuity of species and the shaping of species by natural selection. But, as Darwin was well aware, there were at least two major weaknesses in his argument. Although he hypothesized that variation among individuals is the essential basis for the evolutionary process (natural selection favoring some variants over others), he had no satisfactory way of accounting for the origin of variations—of answering the question "Why is it that individuals are individuals?" Nor could he adequately account for the transmission of traits from one generation to the next.

Mendel and differentiating characters.   The notion prevailing during Darwin's era was that hereditary material is like a fluid. This conception of inheritance meant that every time there was a mating between individuals with contrasting characters or traits (such as white and black hair color) the *hereditary material* would blend, much like different colors of paint, to produce offspring whose characters were intermediate between those of the parents (gray hair color). Generations of such blending would result in a loss of variability and a population completely homogeneous in character. Indeed, many of the complex characters that Darwin and others studied did appear to blend in the offspring populations. Fortunately, Gregor Mendel, an Augustinian monk, chose to examine characters of his pea plants (size, flower color, seed color and texture, and so on) that were dichotomous, or *differentiating* (such as seed color; pea seeds are either yellow or green but no color in between) and that could easily be counted.

Working with these differentiating characters and using a series of breeding experiments, Mendel deduced the nature of the hereditary material and formulated the basic laws of inheritance. There was an ingenuity in the design of his experiments that suggests that Mendel may have had knowledge of the results he would obtain before he actually did his experiments (Bronowski, 1973). Perhaps, as a poor farm boy in what is now Czechoslovakia, he had observed these effects of breeding and was intent now on proving to himself and to his abbot that he was not a complete failure, despite his inability to complete teachers' qualifying examinations at the University of Vienna. Interestingly, after studying inheritance in peas for eight years, he did not embark on any other serious scientific studies but rather became a supporter of radical political positions (Bronowski, 1973).

In his breeding study, Mendel observed that cross-breeding of plants that differed on one of the differentiating characters (tall and short plants, for example) resulted in offspring *all* of which showed only one form of the character (all were tall). There was an apparent dominance of one form of the character over another. The disappearance of the other form of the character was not real, however. Cross-breeding among the offspring plants resulted in a second offspring population three-fourths of which exhibited the dominant form and one-fourth of which showed the previously missing, or recessive, form. This meant that the two forms of the differentiating character retained their purity *and did not blend.* They were transmitted in the germ cells, or gametes, as two different "formative elements," or hereditary factors. Thus, Mendel deduced that every individual has two "formative elements" for each inherited character or trait—one donated by each parent. If they are not alike, one usually dominates over the other. Furthermore, the individual hereditary factors do not change from one generation to the next.

Mendel also found that each pair of differentiating characters that he observed in his experiments (height in plants, color in flowers and seeds) was transmitted independently of the other pairs of characters. In other words, individuals varied in the *combination* of hereditary factors they possessed. All these phenomena, Mendel recognized, could be accounted for by the explanation that the hereditary material is particulate rather than fluid in nature and that the two particles, or formative elements, for a particular differentiating character do not alter each other.

One might have supposed that Mendel's laws of inheritance, accounting, as they did, for the source and means of transmission of character variability, would have been seen as an ideal solution to Darwin's problems. Instead, the climate of scientific opinion at the time of the rediscovery of genetics (the turn of this century) actually led to a decline in the investigation of evolution. Darwin had proposed a theory of heredity in which characters would always be continuous (that is, differences within a population would be small and graded) rather than discontinuous or dichotomous. His supporters had devised a statistical system, called *biometrical analysis,* for the investigation of heredity that was antithetical to Mendel's basic assumptions. Thus, the growing use and success of Mendelian analyses led to a rejection of Darwin's notion of heredity—the biometrical approach—and, strangely enough, to a rejection of the concept of natural selection, as well. The Mendelian laws of inheritance, combined with the notion of gene mutations, appeared to be all that was necessary to account for the variety and evolution of species. Some mutations or combinations of hereditary factors resulted in new species; some did not. Everything could be explained by mutation or recombination of Mendelian factors. Environment (natural selection) caused nothing; genes caused everything. It was as simple as that.

The Synthetic Theory

Although the modern, synthetic theory of evolution involves new concepts of species definition and of the process of natural selection, it is in essence Darwin's original theory combined with Mendelian genetics. Evolutionary change involves changes in the hereditary makeup of a population (the gene pool). Populations are characterized by the relative *percentages* of various kinds and combinations of genes, as inferred from phenotype differences and breeding experiments. Moreover, Mayr (1963) convincingly argued that mutations alone cannot account for the formation of new species—at least not in sexually reproducing populations. It was also mathematically demonstrated that a normally random genetic process such as mutation cannot be responsible for the genetic change, or evolution, of a *population*, except in situations, such as the geographical isolation of a few members from the rest of the population, that maximize sampling error (the Hardy-Weinberg Law).

Evolution, it was reasoned, must involve the one genetic process that is not necessarily random—reproduction. Natural selection thus becomes, in the synthetic theory, any factor that contributes to differential reproduction of the various gene combinations in a population. A species is defined as a population of individuals that have the potential of mating during the natural course of their lives and producing reproductively viable offspring. Species will change in their *genetic* makeup whenever natural selection favors the reproduction of different gene combinations, and a new species will be formed whenever a parent species is physically divided and subjected to differential selection pressures.

Thus, in the synthetic theory, natural selection is the creation of a new adaptive relationship between a population and its environment *not*, as Darwin thought, *through a process of differential survival of individuals but through a process of differential reproduction.*

> The clichés of struggle and survival, even for the professional biologist, have focused attention on secondary aspects of the historical process whereby genetic information accumulates. They have focused it on individuals—and it should be on populations; they have focused it on the avoidance of death (perpetuation of the individual)—and it should be on reproduction (perpetuation of the genotype) [Pittendrigh, 1958, p. 397].

The close association of genetics and evolution led to the creation of a new subdiscipline—population genetics—which has as its focus the search for a more complete understanding of how mutations, selection, population size, environmental conditions, geographical distribution, and other factors concerning a population can influence the evolutionary processes. Population geneticists often speak of a character as inherited; what they mean by this is that the percentage of individuals showing that character in an offspring population can be predicted from knowledge of the percentage of individuals exhibiting the character in the parent population along with knowledge of who mates with whom. This meaning of inheritance says nothing about individual developmental sequences in the ontogeny of the characters and should not be confused, as it often is, with the developmental notion of innate, which means developmentally "fixed" and independent of the environment (Lehrman, 1970; Lerner, 1976).

Perhaps the confusion of the developmental notion *innate* with the genetic notion *inherited* can be traced to the geneticist Bateson's introduction, in the early 1900s, of the term *unit-character* as the name of the hypothesized hereditary material. Unfortunately, this term combined Mendel's "differentiating character"—the observed differences in a character (tallness or shortness in plants, for instance), with his "formative element"—that which is passed on in the germ cells from parent to offspring. The new term gave the impression that the character, and not some hereditary material, was inherited—a notion still found in many discussions of genetics and intelligence. Further contribution to the confusion came from the geneticists' reliance on "differentiating characters" for their investigations of the gene. The ease of counting the individuals possessing these characters and their unambiguous assignment to different groups within a population made experimental manipulations easy and statistical predictions more reliable than developmental investigations.[2] Therefore, as long as Mendelian notions predicted the occurrence of different observed characters within a traditional breeding program, the genes were seen as directly determining the ontogeny of the characters. Indeed, if data from the Mendelian analysis of behavioral characters did not show evidence of predictable major gene effects, it was often concluded that the behavior observed had no genetic origin (Wilcock, 1969).

Gradually, evidence accumulated suggesting that, with few exceptions (notably, those resulting in some abnormal phenotype mutations), the normal occurrence of a character is attributable to the joint action of a number of genes, each making a small contribution to the total phenotype. "All that

[2]Even today, developmental investigations do not enjoy the statistical and experimental sophistication characteristic of genetics. Consequently, there has been a strong tendency among geneticists to ignore development; this was particularly true during the first half of this century. In this vein it is interesting to note that the great pioneering geneticist T. H. Morgan— sometimes considered the father of modern genetics—started his career as an embryologist but became "skeptical of the highly speculative trends in embryology" and quickly turned to and became enamored of the precision and objectivity of genetic investigations (Carlson, 1966).

we can mean when we speak of a gene for pink eyes is, a gene which differentiates a pink eyed fly from a normal one—not a gene which produces pink eyes'' (Sturtevant, 1915, cited in Carlson, 1966, p. 69). Furthermore, the acceptance of Johannsen's 1909 distinction between *genotype* and *phenotype*[3] eventually forced geneticists to recognize that genes and traits are associated through complex networks of developmental pathways. Thus, many modern geneticists fully concede that, although all phenotypic characters, including behavior, have a genetic correlate, or origin, this does not mean that they are independent of specific organism–environment reciprocal interactions for their development. Even the evolutionary biologist must acknowledge that the characteristics of any individual organism within a population are determined by the developmental interactions of the organism with its environment (Simpson, 1958). Or, as the geneticist T. Dobzhansky expressed it,

> Human, as well as animal, behavior is the outcome of a process of develop-ment in which the genes and environment are components of a system of feedback relationships. The same statement can be made equally with re-spect to one's skin color, the shape of one's head, blood chemistry, and somatic, metabolic and mental diseases [1967, p. 43].

In other words, *answers to questions posed by geneticists about populations are not equivalent to answers to questions posed by psychologists about the development of individuals.*

The Search for the Gene

Following the rediscovery of Mendel's work, genetic investigations were of two kinds: assessments of the generality of Mendel's laws of inheri-tance and searches for some material or physical counterpart of his "formative elements." Concrete representation of abstract concepts appears to be an important element in human thought; people often find it difficult to accept the notion that many disciplines are built on foundations of hypothetical con-structs. The postulation of these hypothetical constructs aids in the organiza-tion and coordination of the observed phenomena of the discipline. Genetics is no exception. Even for the modern geneticist, the gene is still, in part, a hypothetical construct.

Early in the history of genetics, advances in the microscopic exami-nation of cells enabled researchers to discover certain elements in the nucleus of the cell that appeared to behave as Mendel's formative elements were thought to behave. These *chromosomes,* so called because they could be

---

[3]*Phenotype* is any *observed* characteristic of the individual (such as blood type, eye color, locomotion patterns, or cell structures). *Genotype* refers to the *inferred* hereditary elements of an individual.

colored with dye, came in pairs and duplicated themselves before a cell divided in two; then each daughter cell received an identical set of chromosomes. Moreover, when the gametes or sex cells were formed, the members of each pair separated and went into different cells, in a manner similar to the hypothesized segregation of the members of a pair of formative elements. Later, with the discovery that members of a pair of chromosomes overlap and exchange material (cross over) before cell division, T. H. Morgan and his colleagues H. J. Muller and A. H. Sturtevant performed a series of ingenious and elegant breeding experiments, the results of which suggested that the formative elements, or *genes* as they were now known, are arranged along the length of a chromosome—much like beads on a string. Each gene was found to have its own particular place or locus on a chromosome, with its "sister" gene (or *allele*) occupying the identical locus on the other member of the chromosome pair.

Continued investigation led to the mapping of gene positions on the chromosomes and the subsequent discovery that three or more different genes might substitute for one another at a locus (multiple alleles). Also, genes at one locus were found to affect the action of genes at another (epistasis). Further evidence confirmed the notion that one gene could be associated with the occurrence of several different phenotypic traits (pleiotropism). In addition, a change in gene structure (mutation) as a result of certain environmental events (X-rays or certain chemicals, for instance) appeared to disrupt the occurrence of the normal phenotype to varying degrees, depending on the overall genetic conditions (expression) and environmental conditions (penetrance). It was also discovered that certain environmental events during development could cause quite different genotypes to exhibit the same phenotypic trait (phenocopy), without any alteration of the genetic structure. Further, the presence of several different genes were shown to be necessary for the expression of most traits (polygenic traits).

The field of genetics rapidly became so sophisticated in its techniques and knowledge of genes that homilies such as "genes set the limits that cannot be exceeded in any environment, but the environment limits the extent to which a genetic potential can be realized," although true, became not only trivial but also misleading. For example, in order to know the potential of any single genotype, researchers would have to raise that genotype from fertilization in every possible environment. It is possible to estimate the genetic potential of a specific genotype by raising it in a random sample of all available environments. However, for many animals, including most species of mammals, even this is an impossible task. And to characterize the limiting effect of any particular environment would require not only detailed knowledge of the peculiarities of the environment but also the results of raising every possible genotype in it. The homily is thus misleading because it suggests that one could actually know the limits of a genetic potential and the effects of all environments on it. Even in the simplest and most manipulable of organisms used for genetic research, these essential criteria have never been fulfilled. We have no means of determining what the potential of any genotype might be or of precisely predicting the effects of any environmental event on the development of an organism. Consequently, questions that depend on such knowledge for their answers are meaningless.

Methods of Behavior-Genetic Analysis

The behavior geneticist is interested primarily in examining the relationship of genetic differences to individual differences in behavior among the members of some population. In order to accomplish this, the researcher must choose behavior patterns that vary among individuals, because, if there are little or no differences among individuals, there will be no way of estimating the relationship of genetic differences to behavior differences. Like most traits, behavior can vary in one of two ways. First, it can vary qualitatively; individuals can easily be assigned to mutually exclusive groups according to their qualitative differences (such as blood type). Second, behavior can vary quantitatively. Individuals are not easily assigned to or divided into mutually exclusive groups on the basis of differences in behavior; rather, behavior seems to vary continuously among individuals (as skin color and height do).

Reflecting this dichotomy in behavioral variability, two distinct research traditions have emerged from behavior-genetic studies—the unifactorial and the multifactorial. The unifactorial approach is to focus on the effects of single genes on behavior, whereas proponents of the multifactorial tradition assume that many genes acting together underlie most behaviors. These two traditions require somewhat different methods for their examinations of behavioral–genetic relationships. The multifactorial approach must rely on sophisticated statistical procedures; the unifactorial approach can rely on the simpler Mendelian techniques.

One common unifactorial method involves comparing the behavior of a normal population with that of a strain, selected from the normal population, carrying a known single-gene mutation. Differences in the behavior of the two populations are assumed to be the consequence of the mutated gene. Wilcock (1969), in a cogently presented review, argued that the vast number of studies demonstrating associations between some single genetic factor and a behavioral trait have focused on trivial pleiotropic effects that are of little relevance to psychological study. Each gene typically is involved in more than one phenotypic characteristic: the gene has pleiotropic effects. The mutation of a single gene generally results in rather gross anatomical and physiological anomalies that in turn can affect behavior simply because they disrupt the organism as a whole. The changes in behavior are pleiotropic effects of the mutated gene. It should not be either surprising or theoretically illuminating that a "sick" or physiologically debilitated animal does not perform in the same way as a "well" animal. For example, there is a severe impairment of human intellectual functioning associated with a condition called *PKU* (phenylketonuria). This condition is believed to be related to a single recessive gene, which when present in both sister chromosomes leads to a reduction in the liver's production of an enzyme called *phenylalanine hydroxase*. As a result, the amino acid phenylalanine, ingested from the diet, is not converted to tyrosine; this failure, in turn, has severe metabolic and anatomical consequences. Restricting the phenylalanine in the diet of infants diagnosed as phenylketonuric significantly reduces the danger of mental retardation. The discovery that this gene is related to intellectual functioning seems trivial in light of its severe consequences for metabolic and anatomical development (recall the distinction between necessary and sufficient conditions that was made in Chapter 2). Thus, the gene is necessary for normal intellectual functioning only through its contribution to the normal metabolism of food; it is not the cause of, or sufficient condition for, intelligence.

Wilcock also noted that, in those unifactorial studies in which the animal was not generally debilitated, behavioral tests were often used that were directly related to the specific, minor anatomical or physiological consequence of the mutation. For instance, is it useful to know that the existence of a gene that disturbs the visual system to such an extent that the animal is virtually blind in normal light is positively correlated with poor performance on a visual-discrimination learning task?

The multifactorial approach also has its problems, although they are not so easily stated. Investigators who use this approach rely on various statistical procedures for the estimation of how much of the differences in individual performance of some behavior can be assigned to genetic differences among the individuals. These *heritability estimates,* as they are called, are useful in animal and plant genetics for the construction and evaluation of breeding programs designed to decrease or increase the frequency of occurrence of some trait in a population. The statistical techniques used depend on a number of important assumptions, the violation of which renders them useless.

The first assumption is that the behavior of each individual can be characterized by a single score or measurement, the value of which is dependent on both genotype and environment. Second, the behavior of a population of individuals can be characterized by group averages and measures of the differences between individual scores (variance measures). This second assumption is usually represented by the equation $\sigma_p^2 = \sigma_g^2 + \sigma_e^2$, which means that the differences (σ^2) in the behavioral phenotype in the population (σ_p^2) are equal to the genotypic (σ_g^2) plus the environmental (σ_e^2) differences among its members. This equation in turn rests on the assumption that the different genetic influences making up σ_g^2 are additive—that is, that there is no interaction among genes. Recently, some geneticists have begun to question whether this last assumption is ever valid. The equation rests on yet another assumption—that the genetic and environmental circumstances of the individual are additive, independent, and not covarying. This last assumption is extensively violated in human genetic research (Cavalli-Sforza & Bodmer, 1971). That is to say, humans do not mate randomly but instead tend to mate with people who are like them in background, socioeconomic class, education, and so forth.

Despite the problems it presents regarding the validity of these assumptions, this equation can be used to derive a common heritability estimate (h^2) in the following way: $h^2 = \sigma_g^2/(\sigma_g^2 + \sigma_e^2) = \sigma_g^2/\sigma_p^2$. This last equation gives an estimate of the proportion of individual differences in phenotype that is due to differences in genotype. Note that, in animals, heritability is never estimated for whole behaviors or behavioral complexes such as aggression, intelligence, or fear but only for one feature of the pattern, such as the frequency, *or* the intensity, *or* the duration of fighting *in a specific situation*.

In order to get the necessary estimates of the separate genetic and environmental influences on a score, special breeding procedures must be used. By mating only brothers and sisters for some 20 to 30 generations, investigators can produce an inbred strain in which all members possess the same genotype, much like identical twins. Because the members of an inbred strain are genetically identical, any differences in their scores on some test must be due to environmental influences. By comparing the differences in scores of an inbred strain with the differences in scores of a normal, or randomly bred, population, researchers obtain an estimate of h^2.

Using the example of fighting in mice, the logic of the h^2 estimate is as follows.

1. The score differences, on some aggression test, for a randomly bred population are assumed to reflect both genotypic and environmental influences. This is expressed by the equation $\sigma_p^2 = \sigma_g^2 + \sigma_e^2$.
2. The score differences, on the same test, for an inbred strain are assumed to reflect only environmental influences. This is expressed σ_e^2.
3. One estimates the genetic component of the score difference by subtracting the result of step 2 from the result of step 1: $\sigma_p^2 - \sigma_e^2 = \sigma_g^2$.
4. Finally, one estimates the heritability of aggression in mice by dividing the result of step 3 by the result of step 1: $\sigma_g^2/\sigma_p^2 = h^2$.

Because it is morally and ethically wrong to create inbred strains of human beings, investigators of human genetics have had to rely on some less-than-optimal techniques for their estimations of environmental influences. The most powerful technique is the comparison of identical twins that have been reared apart. Indeed, such studies formed the foundation of Jensen's argument about the heritability of intelligence. However, more careful examination of these studies (Bronfenbrenner, 1972; Kamin, 1974) revealed major inconsistencies and contradictions in the data as well as the fact that the twins were often reared by close relatives living in the same or similar neighborhoods. Given the structure of human society, it is unlikely that any group of twins would ever be reared apart in environments different enough to even vaguely represent the diversity of environmental conditions found in typical societies. Indeed, the difficulty of adequately meeting the requirements of modern genetics has prompted two geneticists to conclude that there cannot be a science of human behavior genetics at this time (Bodmer & Cavalli-Sforza, 1970).

Even if it were possible to obtain valid estimates of the heritability of any human trait, these estimates would offer little in the way of information about the development of the trait. As Hirsch (1970) has indicated, heritability is a convenient but fleeting *statistic*, not a measure of genetic determination. Any heritability estimate is completely dependent on the environmental circumstances and genetic differences present at the time of testing in those specific populations examined. Whether high or low, the heritability estimate is not valid for other populations, or for the same population given different environmental circumstances, or even for the same population measured at different developmental stages or in different generations. The interest generated by the Jensen thesis reflects an ignorance of modern quantitative genetics.

Molecular Genetics and Development

The recent association of the molecule DNA with the gene concept and the subsequent emergence of the field of molecular or chemical genetics have made available new ways of studying the developmental pathways associating genotypes with phenotypes.

Molecular geneticists are currently pursuing two lines of investigation. The first is concerned with the redefinition of Mendelian genetics in terms of physicochemical events and structures characteristic of cells. Although this may appear to be an excellent case of reduction in the sense discussed in Chapter Two, many biologists and philosophers (Hull, 1972) have demonstrated that before the relationship between molecular and Mendelian genetics could be satisfactorily stated there would have to be an exchange of concepts and notions by the two approaches. As a result there would be no reduction but a growing-together, or synthesis, of the two subdisciplines.

The second line of investigation traces the biochemical developmental pathways leading from the activities of DNA in the cell nucleus to the appearance of phenotypic traits. Of course, this endeavor is in its infancy and only some of the very simplest of pathways have been determined, but it does promise to be a significant source of information about developmental phenomena. Unfortunately, the emergence of these molecular investigations of development has prompted a resurgence of the preformationist and pre-determinist notions of development. However, there is nothing inherent in the concepts of molecular genetics that warrants such a revival of outdated notions about development. Indeed, molecular models of the gene provide for environmental influence. Moreover, as research in this field accumulates, notions about levels of organization in the developmental pathways relating DNA activity to behavior become more salient, and explanations of proper functioning at the behavioral level are increasingly seen to be dependent on, but not reducible to, an understanding of the functioning of the biochemistry of cells.

For example, Ginsburg (1971) reports that a single-gene mutation in the C57BL strain of mice is associated with the occurrence of seizures in response to loud noises. However, these audiogenic seizures occur only if the mutant C57BL mice were exposed to loud noises sometime during day 18 or 19 after birth. The nonmutant C57BL mice are relatively seizure resistant. Thus, an early experience with noise (which does not produce a seizure at that time) is responsible for the development of seizure proneness only in mutant C57BL mice. Further, the development of seizure proneness in mutants is dependent on the timing of the early noise experience; exposure at any other time except during day 18 or 19 has no effect. Biochemical analysis revealed that a particular enzyme is rapidly increasing at the crucial time. The enzyme (glutamic acid decarboxylase—GAD) controls a process (the decarboxylation of glutamic acid) that results in the formation of a chemical (GABA) that is involved in the inhibition of neural activity. The presentation of loud noises to the animal during the period in which GAD is rapidly increasing significantly alters the final resting level of GAD (either raising or lowering it). Early exposure to loud noises may thus produce seizure-prone adults by altering the GABA levels in the brain. Indeed, experimenters subsequently confirmed this hypothesis by injecting nonmutant mice with chemicals that alter only GABA levels. These mice exhibited seizure proneness even though they had not been previously exposed to loud noises.

Thus, the disruption of a biochemical process can have ramifications at all of the various systemic levels of the organism. Using biochemical information, researchers could develop phenocopies of either seizure-prone or seizure-resistant characteristics in mice having the opposite genetic predispositions. Moreover, these alterations could be accomplished through either environmental or biochemical manipulation. Biochemical processes are basic components of the systems of organization within the individual. Therefore, knowledge of molecular genetics and biology can be an important tool for the understanding of developmental processes. But the pathway associating a biochemical process with a behavior passes through several levels of organization, and at each level there is ample opportunity for environmental influence. Indeed, the more complex the level of organization, the more extensive the environmental influence.

Genetics and Conception

Molecular genetics itself begins with the processes necessary for conception. The female and male of sexually reproducing species each have specialized cells (gametes) that possess only half the total number of chromosomes typical of that species. For example, whereas each human cell contains 46 chromosomes, human gametes (egg and sperm cells) contain only 23. The

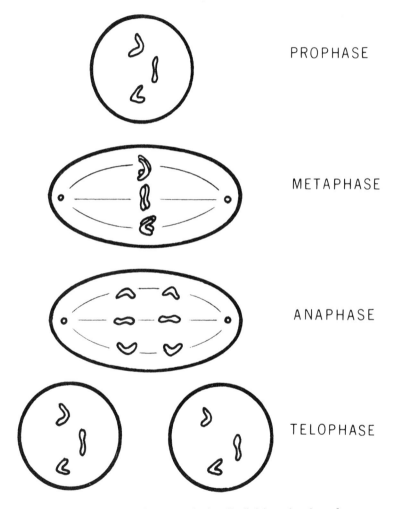

PROPHASE

METAPHASE

ANAPHASE

TELOPHASE

Figure 4-1. Mitosis, or typical cell division, involves four stages. In prophase, the cell grows. Then the chromosomes duplicate, and two poles form at opposite ends of the cell (metaphase). The duplicated chromosomes separate and migrate toward different poles (anaphase). Finally, the cell wall involutes, forming two separate daughter cells (telophase).

formation of these gametes occurs via a special kind of cell division (meiosis), which, instead of duplicating the number of chromosomes for each new daughter cell (as in the usual cell division—mitosis), halves them. Moreover,

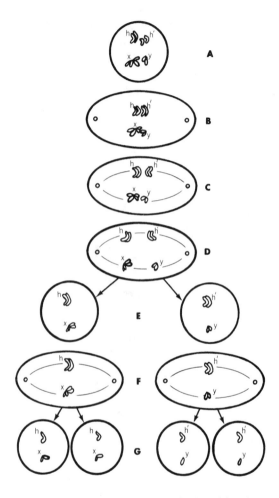

Figure 4-2.   Meiosis is a special kind of cell division that results in the formation of sperm or egg cells. Each homologous chromosome (for example, h and h'), including the sex-determining chromosomes (x and y), first duplicates its DNA (A). Then, the homologous pairs and their duplications line up in the center of the cell as the opposite poles form (B), and each member of a pair along with its duplication, moves to an opposite pole (C and D). The cell wall involutes, forming two daughter cells (E). In the second division, the duplicated chromosomes separate (F) to produce a total of four daughter cells (G), each containing half the total number of chromosomes of the precursor cell (A).

because each chromosome can behave independently of the others during cell division, each gamete produced will have a different combination of chromosomes and, consequently, of genes.

Conception, or fertilization, occurs when the chromosomes of a male gamete enter the nucleus of a female gamete, forming a new cell (zygote) possessing the number of chromosomes typical of that species. Following conception, the zygote begins to grow and divides (via mitosis) into two cells, each of which divides, yielding four cells, then 16 cells, and so on. Each new daughter cell formed by these divisions contains identical reproductions of the original chromosomes. Biochemical research has shown that the primary constituent of the chromosomes is the molecule deoxyribonucleic acid—DNA.

The gene and DNA.   In the early 1950s, J. Watson and F. Crick proposed a model for the structure of the DNA molecule that would account for its identical duplication during cell division. Watson and Crick characterized the DNA molecule as a long chain composed of two strands of sugarphosphate molecules linked together, in a twisting parallel, or double helix, by a series of chemical bases (adenine, cytosine, thymine, and guanine) attached to one side of each strand. Although the order of the bases could vary along the DNA molecule, the bases could connect the two strands in only two ways. Thymine could unite chemically only with adenine, and guanine only with cytosine; no other connections were possible. In this way the order of bases on one strand controlled the order of bases on the other strand. For example, if one strand contained the base sequence CTCATC, the other strand must contain the sequence GAGTAG, or else the two strands would not unite to form a DNA molecule.

The double-stranded nature of the DNA molecule and the restriction on the pairing of the bases make it possible for DNA to be duplicated exactly. During the process of cell division, the two strands of DNA unravel and separate. The nucleus of the cell usually contains an excess of nucleotides (sugarphosphate molecules attached to a single base); as soon as the strands begin separating, duplicate strands are built by the attachment of these excess nucleotides to each of the separating strands. In this way, two identical and separate molecules of DNA are formed. After cell division, each becomes part of the nucleus of one of the two newly formed daughter cells.

As the zygote continues to undergo the cell division that results in the formation of an embryo, two complex processes occur. First, the cells begin to take on different shapes and functions. These *differentiated* cells differ from one another not only in their morphological appearance but also in their biochemical constitution and their physiological processes, even though they contain identical genetic material! Second, as more and more cells are produced, cell differentiation begins to occur in an orderly way, at specific times and in specific places. In other words, patterns of cells are formed (a process known as *morphogenesis*). It is these two processes—morphogenesis and differentiation—that concern molecular geneticists when they are pursuing developmental questions.

DNA and proteins. Whereas the "gene" studied by Mendelian geneticists is typically associated with gross anatomical or behavioral characters, DNA is involved primarily in the production of proteins. Of course, proteins are the most important class of physicochemical substances in a cell. They are large molecules made of folded filaments called *polypeptides.* Each kind of protein has a different function in a cell, determined largely by its physicochemical shape and properties. Proteins are the primary building material for all the structures of a cell. However, the most common and important function of proteins is carried out by those proteins that are enzymes. Enzymes regulate the rate of physicochemical reactions in a cell, providing the energy necessary for the cell to grow and perform its biochemical and physiological functions. As a rule, each step in every biochemical process in a cell or organism requires a specific enzyme for its occurrence. And the association of a particular DNA "code" with a behavioral character involves a complex network of biochemical and physiological events, the nature of which is in part determined by the organism's peculiar environmental circumstances.

The construction of a specific protein is governed by the order (which is next to which) of the bases on one of the strands of the DNA double helix. Thus, the sequence of bases on a strand of DNA is a "code" for a particular protein. Three adjacent bases (a triplet) correspond to one particular amino acid, and each polypeptide filament of protein consists of a linear series, or chain, of these amino acids. In all, there are about 20 different kinds of amino acids used in the construction of polypeptide filaments.

If you think of proteins as sentences and amino acids as words that can be combined in various numbers and ways, you can easily see that the very large number of proteins necessary for cellular function can be produced from only 20 amino acids. Because three adjacent bases on the DNA code form a specific amino acid, the order of the bases will control the order of the amino acids in a polypeptide chain and, consequently, the kind of protein produced.

Most of the cell's activity and protein synthesis take place in the cytoplasm outside of the nucleus, yet the DNA of most organisms is confined to the nucleus. How is the DNA's information for protein synthesis transmitted to the relevant structure (ribosomes) in the cytoplasm? It was discovered that there is a special kind of ribonucleic acid (m-RNA) that appears in the nucleus and can move into the cytoplasm. This m-RNA is composed of a single strand of nucleotides and can be constructed so as to copy all or part of a single strand of DNA. The information about the amino-acid sequence of a particular protein is thus *transcribed* by the construction of m-RNA, which then passes out to the cytoplasm.

Before amino acids can be joined to form polypeptide chains, they must be activated by attachment to certain phosphoric-acid groups. These "activated" amino acids then become attached, via this acid group, to a second kind of RNA—transfer, or t-, RNA. Transfer RNA then has three nucleotides at one end and an activated amino acid at the other end. This "open" nucleotide triplet allows t-RNA to attach to the appropriate part of m-RNA. The piecing-together of t-RNA and m-RNA for the production of a polypeptide sequence takes place on the ribosome. Once an amino acid has been placed in the sequence, the t-RNA is released and returns to the cytoplasm to attach to another appropriate "activated" amino acid. After an m-RNA sequence has been completely translated into a protein, it is released from the ribosome and broken down into individual nucleotides.

The regulation of protein synthesis is assumed to be the basis for the development of different cells from the same DNA. That is, as a result of differential protein synthesis, different enzymes are produced that enable different chemical reactions to occur, leading eventually to morphologically, biochemically, and physiologically differentiated cells.

Two men—F. Jacob and J. Monod (1961)—working on the enzyme production of the intestinal bacterium E. coli, proposed a model of gene structure and activity that could account for certain forms of cell differentiation during development. They suggested that gene activity on the molecular level consists of three factors:

1. a structural factor, which contains the triplet codes for the amino-acid sequences necessary for the construction of a protein;
2. an operator factor, which is close in space to the structural factor and which can induce ("turn on") the structural factor to form sequences of m-RNA; and
3. a regulator factor, which need not be spatially linked to the operator but which produces a protein that combines with the operator to block or repress m-RNA formation.

The protein formed by this regulator factor also has the ability to combine with certain other chemical substances. What this means is that certain chemicals, called inducers, entering the cell from the outside, or even the products of other structural factors within the cell, can combine with the regulator protein and prevent it from inhibiting the operator factor. The operator factor thus activates the structural factor, and m-RNA is constructed. For more complex organisms that are composed of cells in which the DNA is confined to a nucleus, the Jacob-Monod model needs some modification. The activity of DNA production of m-RNA in complex organisms is directly influenced by specific biochemical substances such as hormones and cellular enzymes. Because these substances can regulate genetic activity directly, the need for a separate regulator factor appears to be associated only with the DNA activity of simpler organisms.

A
Transcription of DNA Strand to Messenger RNA

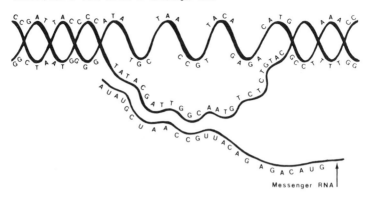

Messenger RNA

B
Translation of Messenger RNA into Protein

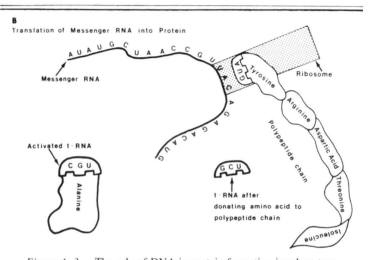

Figure 4–3. The role of DNA in protein formation involves two kinds of processes. In transcription (A), a section of DNA unravels, and free nucleotides (guanine, cytosine, adenine, and uracil) bind with their counterparts on the DNA strand to form a strand of messenger RNA (m-RNA). After separating from the DNA, the m-RNA passes out of the nucleus into the cytoplasm and couples with the ribosome. Here, the second process—translation (B)— takes place. Each combination of three nucleotides on the m-RNA specifies a particular amino acid. The appropriate amino acid is brought to the ribosome by transfer RNA (t-RNA). Each t-RNA consists of a combination of three nucleotides that will bind only with a particular amino acid and only with a particular set of three nucleotides on m-RNA. Thus, the sequence GUA on t-RNA can bind only with the amino acid tyrosine and the sequence UAC on m-RNA. By "reading" along the nucleotide sequence of the m-RNA, the ribosome, with the help of t-RNA, builds the polypeptide chain of a protein.

Genes and the Environment

Remember, for the geneticist the environment is everything external to the DNA or genome (complete set of genes) of an individual that mediates and influences the timing and concentration of enzyme production involved in phenotypic development. The environment includes the substances in the cell that are manufactured by that cell, or that are incorporated from other cells, tissues, and organs, or that are the metabolites of ingested food. All these substances together can be considered the chemical milieu influencing DNA regulation of protein synthesis. The Jacob-Monod model of gene action details the means by which alterations in the chemical milieu can lead to changes in the amounts and kinds of enzymes produced by a cell and, consequently, its biochemical properties. Of course, changes in the biochemical properties of nerve cells or cells involved in hormone secretion may ultimately be reflected in changes in behavior.

In contrast, the environment for the psychologist is all of those factors (physical energies, material objects, social companions, and so on) outside of the boundary of the individual's skin. These environmental factors can influence the activity of DNA and the cell primarily through their effects on the individual's internal chemical milieu. In multicellular, and in many noncellular, organisms, specific organs or organelles have evolved to enhance and control the effects of the environment on the chemical milieu. These special structures are called *biological transducers* because they change environmental energies (light, sound, gravitation, and so on) into biochemical substances. As yet, science is far from understanding, even for the simplest of organisms, the sequence of events that alters the chemical milieu, which, in turn, affects enzyme production during development. It should be recognized, however, that the environment and experiences of an individual can be important influences on the behavioral organization of the individual, precisely as a consequence of the individual's molecular biological organization. The work of both the molecular geneticist and the developmental psychologist contributes to the understanding of behavioral development.

Summary

We have tried to show that the interrelationship of genetics, evolution, and development is more complex than one might deduce from conventional wisdom. One branch of genetics—population genetics—is closely associated with the study of evolution. At one time, genetic and evolutionary hypotheses were considered competing explanations of the same phenomena, but modern evolutionary theory successfully integrates them as complements. For example, the conception of genes as particulate units of inheritance capable of exact self-replication offers a mechanism that can be used to support the notions of evolutionary continuity and relationship. Natural selection is now seen as whatever brings about differential reproduction of genes from one generation to the next.

Because of the nature of their concepts and methods, population geneticists and other biologists interested in the process of evolution are restricted to the study of groups. Their contribution to the study of individual behavioral development is limited to the posing of interesting questions for developmental analysis and to suggestions that certain developmental pathways or strategies may not be involved in the development of some behavior. Population genetics cannot provide answers to developmental questions, nor can it specify the pathways involved in the development of any character, including behavior.

Molecular genetics, on the other hand, involves the study of individuals. Unlike their colleagues in population genetics, molecular geneticists are concerned with genes as biochemical units in the cells of individuals. They study the processes through which genes contribute to the functioning of cells and to the development of new cells. The work of the molecular geneticist is qualitatively continuous with that of the developmental psychologist because they both seek to understand the functioning and development of individuals. However, the levels of organization on which the members of these two disciplines focus their attention are so different that examples of meaningful contact between them can be found only in relatively trivial, although dramatic, pleiotropic single-gene effects. Understanding of the developmental pathways of behavioral organization will require knowledge of the ways in which individual experiences affect the biochemistry of cells as well as knowledge of the biochemical activities themselves.

We have argued that evolutionary investigations cannot supply answers to developmental questions but that taking an evolutionary perspective can suggest new questions and provide a fresh way of posing old questions. In the next chapter, we will examine some of the ways in which an evolutionary perspective, particularly as articulated in ethology, has been brought to bear on questions belonging to developmental psychology.

Chapter Five

Animal Behavior, Ethology, and Human Development

Two Orientations to the Study of Animal Behavior

As you now know, scientists can be identified by their orientation to their work as well as by the specific content of their studies. Scientists studying animal behavior are no exception. Lehrman (1971) described two rather divergent orientations characteristic of people interested in animal behavior. He argued that scientists who share the natural-history orientation are interested in behavior patterns that enable animals to cope with the circumstances of their natural environments. These scientists tend to study an animal's behavior in the setting within which it evolved, or at least they aim to relate the results of their investigations to that setting. They also focus their attention on behavior patterns that allow the posing of questions and hypotheses about survival value.

The implicit goal of the natural-history orientation is an understanding of how the animal's behavior is related to evolutionary processes. The theory of evolution accounts for similarity and diversity among life forms with the notions of descent from common ancestors and the consequences of natural selection; each species of animal is thought to represent a solution to the problems posed by a unique set of ecological conditions. Thus, scientists with a natural-history orientation are interested in the contribution of the animal's behavior to its meeting the problems of its world.

We cannot stress too strongly that it is the animal and *its* world that concern scientists who have a natural-history orientation to animal behavior. Such scientists tend to express a genuine wonder and curiosity about animals and their worlds and are ever alert against possible incursions of notions or questions reflecting specifically human concerns and issues into their studies of animal behavior.

Scientists having an anthropocentric orientation, on the other hand, study the behavior of animals mainly as a means of defining and examining what they consider to be general laws of behavior. These general laws are discerned by procedures that enable the scientist to gain control over the animal's behavior and to predict its frequency of occurrence. Scientists adopting the anthropocentric orientation have as their explicit goal the application of these animal-derived general laws to human behavior. Their goal is not to understand the animal and its world but to use the animal as a tool for the investigation of specifically human problems in psychology.

Obviously, the anthropocentric orientation has the greater appeal, in light of the troubles that plague human society. This favored status becomes particularly apparent when expensive animal-behavior research must rely on public support. Support will often be contingent upon the degree to which the research results will be applicable to human problems. As a result of this pressure to focus on human issues and problems, even the results of animal-behavior studies conducted within the natural-history orientation may be forced into discussions representing an anthropocentric orientation—witness the explosion of popular and "scientific" accounts of the nature of human behavior based on the results of natural-history studies of animal behavior (for example, Ardrey, *The Territorial Imperative*, 1966; Lorenz, *On Aggression*, 1966; Morris, *The Naked Ape*, 1967; Tiger, *Men in Groups*, 1969).

Although the anthropocentric orientation has some merit and consensual support, we confess a greater sympathy with the natural-history orientation. It is this latter orientation, most often associated with the study of animal behavior called *ethology*, that we feel can be of more value in the study of human psychological development. Although this may seem paradoxical in light of the goal of the anthropocentric orientation (that is, to discover general laws of behavior that can be used in the resolution of human behavioral problems), we hope to show in this chapter that it is not.

The Natural-History Orientation and the Ethological Approach

Early Ethology

Although the roots of ethology can be traced to pre-Darwinian biologists interested in natural history (Jaynes, 1969), it was only with the writings of such self-acknowledged ethologists as Lorenz, Tinbergen, Baerends, and Kortlandt during the period 1935 to 1951 that ethology coalesced into a coherent discipline. Many of the early ethological writings were attempts to distinguish the ideas of the new discipline from the older, mechanistic and vitalistic ideas about animal behavior.

Mechanism and vitalism. Mechanists argued that an animal's behavior consists of simple stimulus–response reflexes, some of which may be elaborated into more complex behavior by Pavlovian conditioning, by stimulus-controlled chains of responses, or by trial-and-error learning. The observations and experiments conducted by ethologists showed, however, that an animal's behavioral repertoire consists of patterns, more complex than reflexes, that occur in the absence of Pavlovian conditioning, practice, or trial-and-error learning. In this belief, the ethologists were in agreement with the vitalists.

The vitalists, however, argued that an animal's behavior not only is more than reflexes and conditioning but also is organized and regulated by the goal achieved through the performance of the behavior. For the vitalist, at the core of these complex behaviors are *instincts*—driving, purposive forces. That is to say, the cause of an instinctive behavior was thought to be the achievement of the goal or consequence of that instinct. Thus, care of the young was simultaneously the cause (instinctive drive) and consequence (purposive goal) of the performance of maternal behavior in mammals. The ethologists sought to distinguish between instinct as a cause in the vitalistic, purposive sense and instinct as a description of certain specific characteristics of the behavioral event.

As a result of ethological research, it was discerned that those behaviors of animals that historically have been classified as instinctive are not guided, as the vitalists proposed, by purposes or functional consequences. Early ethological work seemed to demonstrate that the performance of an instinctive behavior is terminated not by the achievement of its purposive goal but rather by performance of the action itself. Lorenz (1937/1957) hypothesized that the performance of an instinctive act is energized by a specific energy that is released by the appropriate environmental stimuli and depleted by the performance itself. Thus, the mother rat crouches over her young not because the young can thereby suckle but because of the activation of the neural control of crouching by a specific energy source that was released by specific stimuli from the young (such as squealing). She ceases to crouch when this energy has been consumed or when the releasing stimulus has been removed—not necessarily when the young are full.

Although the constructs and details of the early ethological position are demonstrably wrong (see, for example, Beer, 1973), the antivitalist conclusion stands. The animal's performance of instinctive, functionally important behaviors is not caused or guided by its "knowledge" of their consequences. There is no empirical basis for characterizing the animal's behavior as purposive.

Natural selection and animal behavior. The ethologists did more than point out the weaknesses inherent in the mechanistic and vitalistic positions. Their major contribution was the establishment, as a basic feature of their discipline and as a viable foundation for the study of behavior in general, the fact that animal behavior is structured by natural selection. It was argued that, because an animal's behavior is like its organs, in the sense that it is structured by the requirements of survival, it can be studied by essentially the same methods that had been used so successfully in the study of organs. This, of course, was the position taken originally by Darwin.

Ethologists' generalization of evolutionary thought to behavior was put into practice in several ways. For example, the phylogenetic history of behavior patterns was ascertained through comparison of closely related species (Lorenz, 1941/1971a; Tinbergen, 1959). Behavior was scrutinized for its relevance to survival in a way that had been reserved for such anatomical characteristics as the shape of a bird's beak (Lack, 1947; Tinbergen, 1965). Systematic study of the social and ecological consequences of behavior began to be employed (Cullen, 1957; Tinbergen, Broekhuysen, Feekes, Houghton, Kruuk, & Szulc, 1962). Ethologists also studied the causation and development of the animal's behavioral repertoire by means of systematic experimental manipulations. These studies revealed that behavior was often not simply a reaction to a stimulus but, rather, dependent on a specifiable condition, or *state*, of the animal. Furthermore, when behavior was a reaction to stimulation, it was usually elicited by only a subset of all the available stimulus cues; each separate behavior was associated with a different subset of the potential cues.

Also underlying all ethological research is the basic assumption that the understanding of any behavior can be achieved only within the context of a thorough knowledge of the animal's environment and full behavioral repertoire. Thus, ethology maintains a strong natural-history orientation to the study of animal behavior.

As ethology took form as a discipline, it generated a number of theories and theoretical constructs designed to describe and explain why the animal behaves when and where it does. These constructs were concerned with, among other things, the specificity of stimulus cues (the constructs *sign stimulus* and *innate releasing mechanism* are examples) and the stereotypy of some behavior patterns (an example is the construct *fixed action pattern*). However, it is not these theories or constructs that are of value for the study of human development. For, as Tinbergen (1968) argued, the theories and constructs of ethology have changed and will continue to change with further research (see Beer, 1973). According to Tinbergen, those interested in the integration of ethology and human psychology should attend to the approach (attitudes, methods, concerns) of ethology rather than to its theories or constructs.

The Ethological Approach

As we have indicated, the ethological approach begins with systematic descriptions of the animal's behavior in the setting within which it continues to evolve. Once the animal's behavioral repertoire has been constructed and its general environmental circumstances described, questions are posed for experimental investigation. In the normal sequence of events, an ethologist's questions about behavior arise directly from the examination of a particular animal's behavioral repertoire in its natural setting. The answers obtained through such experimental investigations are always relevant—at least to the animal studied.

Although the specifics of the questions posed by the ethologists are addressed to the particular characteristics of the animal studied, they are always derivatives of the four types of questions we described in Chapter Three: causal, functional, evolutionary, and developmental.

Finally, each aspect of the ethological approach is guided by the evolutionary perspective that the behavior of an animal is as integral a component of its adjustment to environmental circumstances as any other of its systems. This is true, by extension, of the behavior of humans, as well.

Contributions of the Natural-History Orientation to the Study of Human Development

We would argue along with Ambrose (1968) that the natural-history orientation to the study of animal behavior has made at least four contributions to the study of human psychological development. These include the development of new research techniques, the clarification of concepts used in the study of human behavioral development, the identification of special features of human development, and the identification of issues in human development that need study.

The Development of New Research Techniques

Description. The study of animal behavior has been a source of novel research techniques that have been fruitfully applied to the study of human development. Recent studies examining what children *do* rather than what parents, children, or others *say* they do owe much of their methodology to ethological studies of animals (Blurton Jones, 1974; Richards & Bernal, 1972). This is not to say that developmental psychologists never used to directly observe children or that they would never have thought of doing so had it not been for the example of animal behaviorists. People have probably always observed one another reflectively, but observation is an active process that can be accomplished in several ways. What ethology has provided is not merely a rejuvenation of the old idea of observation as a necessary part of science; it is a new way of observing behavior.

It is quite possible for people to use highly complex categories in describing behavior without attending to, or even being aware of, the steps through which the categories have been formed. Phenomenologically, the complex behavioral category is "seen" directly, although in fact it is derived from a series of mental manipulations involving the ordering, classification, and predictior of incoming information. One can quite readily demonstrate this both by questioning one's own experience and by examining a standard method adopted in many studies of human behavior. Consider the term *aggressive*—a descriptive label used frequently in both scientific and lay circles. You have probably had occasion to apply the term to someone, yet, if pressed would probably have found it difficult to spell out all the steps you had taken to arrive at that description; you might offer a definition, such as "the person is likely to hurt someone" (also not an observable), or you might relate an anecdote. Further, you will find that others will, at least apparently, know what you are talking about and be able to use the same label in more or less the same way! Therefore, we can conclude that people are capable of forming complexly derived descriptive categories of behavior in an apparently immediate fashion, that they can use these categories reliably, and that different people can agree on the use of such higher-order descriptive terms. There are some problems, however. First, higher-order descriptive terms may be used in more than one way: two individuals may be classified as aggressive but each for a different reason (consider a hoodlum and a corporate executive). This may or may not be fully realized by users of the term. Second, although people can agree on the use of terms of this nature, they may also disagree or, worse, only seem to agree (for example, when male and female children are called *aggressive*, is the same thing meant in each case?).

There is a tradition of descriptive research within human psychology that is based on our ordinary practice of describing one another with higher-order terms. Before these terms can be used in a study, special procedures are employed to assure that they can be used reliably to describe events and that different individuals can come to use them in the same way. The most widely used procedure is to have more than one observer of the same events. Observers typically go through a period of training, during which they learn the language to be employed in the study, before the study begins. By correlating the data obtained by two or more independent observers, the researcher can assess the degree of interobserver reliability for each behavioral category.

This reliability procedure assures that the observers are responding to something in the behavior of their subjects. However, it does not allow, or even aim to allow, documentation of the steps taken by the observers in reaching their descriptive categories. It can be argued that, for some purposes, this doesn't matter. However, communication can break down entirely when the descriptions, applied very reliably by the observers within a study, are used by others who did not participate in the reliability training sessions. That is, because the understanding imparted in reliability training is primarily intuitive, it can be achieved only through shared experience; overt instruction will not work. Truly independent replication of these studies—an absolute prerequisite for the establishment of scientific knowledge—is therefore ruled out.

Perhaps because application of higher-order descriptive terms to animals can quickly lead to anthropomorphism and confusion, ethologists have been very concerned with using objective terms for their primary descriptive data. In this context, *objective* means capable of being transmitted without confusion to others who have not trained with the observer. Descriptive categories are either movement patterns (such as smiling) or patterns with unambiguous consequences (such as nest-building). It is possible to draw, photograph, or tape-record the sort of behavior patterns that make up the primary descriptive categories of ethologists; it is not possible to photograph aggression or other higher-order descriptive categories. The motion photography of a fight scene is only a representation or index of aggression.

Although ethologists also use higher-order categories, they construct them from the observable categories used in their descriptive records. The steps in the construction process must be specifiable and open to inspection and verification. A substantial portion of ethological research is devoted to the methodological issues attending this process (see, for example, Slater, 1973).

Some recent work on the human mother–infant relationship provides one indication that developmental psychologists may also usefully employ ethological methods of description. Using observable behavioral categories, such as crying, puckering, smiling, touching, and kissing, Blurton Jones and Leach (1972) described the interactions between young children who were participating in a play group and their mothers during the separation and greeting at the beginning and end of each play session. They went on to construct higher-order categories from their primary data through the statistical technique of factor analysis and were able to show several interesting things about human attachment. First, earlier notions of attachment (Bowlby, 1969) had been based on the assumption that crying on the departure of the mother and smiling at the mother on her arrival are two of the several covarying indicators that the young child is attached to the mother. Yet the children in this study who cried were not more likely to smile than those who did not. Further, Blurton Jones and Leach found that crying per se does not lead to greater maternal proximity. Mothers of young (under 2½ years) children touched and were in other ways more responsive to criers than to noncriers, but this relationship was reversed for older children. Thus, the child's social bond with its mother cannot be characterized by a unitary attachment factor having a clear set of behavioral indicators, as was hypothesized on the basis of earlier work.

In a different observational study of attachment, J. W. Anderson (1972) described the behavior of toddlers in a park in the presence of a stationary mother. One of his discoveries was that toddlers spend more time going away from their mothers than in returning to them; these same toddlers would, however, return to their mothers without any active retrieval on the part of the mother. This unpredicted observation points to the prematurity of such higher-order descriptive labels as *attachment, independence,* and *security.* These constructs are so broad that they don't allow for a distinction between a child who is "attached but secure" and a child who is "unattached and independent." In other words, Anderson's toddlers could be described either as highly interested in proximity to the mother (that is, attached) but secure enough also to express their interest in the physical environment, or as relatively less interested in proximity to mother (unattached) and interested in exploration of the physical environment.

By preserving a quantitative record of observables, Anderson, like Blurton Jones and Leach, allows others the opportunity of constructing complex categories that are closely associated with what the individuals actually are doing. Researchers who begin with complex descriptive categories, on the other hand, may never discover that the categories are imperfectly defined, or even faulty.

As the sheer amount of what is known about mother–infant social behavior is increased by ethology-like descriptive studies, new higher-order categories for describing the mother–infant relationship will be introduced, or the characteristics defining the older categories will be changed. For example, there is no good reason to continue using the concept of attachment to refer to a property of the infant; it may better describe the interactive relationship between the infant and its mother. Anderson suggests that the boundary within which a toddler may freely move away from the mother is mutually agreed upon for each mother–toddler dyad. The active, as opposed to the permissive, role of the mother in the child's early social behavior has been emphasized in other contexts. Klaus and Kennell (1970) for example, have shown that the *mother's* attachment to her premature infant is disturbed by enforced separation during hospital care and by her fear of the infant's death; her attachment is a prerequisite to satisfactory social development in the infant.

Analysis of social behavior. Because ethologists are concerned primarily with social behavior, they have developed sophisticated statistical procedures for analyzing behavioral interactions. One focus has been on what usually falls under the rubric of *communication*—namely, the effects of one individual's behavior on the behavior of a second individual.

The most productive procedure for analyzing animal communication is *sequence analysis.* Sequence analysis is concerned with the chronological sequence of events; applied to social interactions, it is concerned with the sequential occurrence of behavior patterns in two individuals. Given that animal A has done one thing, what is the next thing that animal B will do? With a relatively large sample of behavioral records, it can be determined whether behavior exhibited by one animal is nonrandomly related to the next behavior performed by a second animal. If so, it can be concluded that animal B has responded to animal A.

Dingle's (1969) study of the mantis shrimp provides a good example of how social communication among animals can be discovered with this technique. For instance, Dingle found that a "lunge" by one mantis shrimp will most probably be followed by a "coil" from the second shrimp and is unlikely to be followed at greater than chance level by most other patterns within the animal's behavioral repertoire. Similar examples could be extracted from studies of a wide range of invertebrate and vertebrate species, including humans (Bakeman, 1975; Lytton & Zwirner, 1975). The method is therefore quite generalizable, even though the nature of communication mechanisms differs dramatically among species (Marler & Hamilton, 1966).

Studies of animal communication start with descriptions of social-behavior units as they can be observed in single individuals. At this level of inquiry, researchers are interested in communicative patterns and in the nature of the information that is transmitted. A second, less clearly understood focus in the study of animal social behavior begins with an interest in phenomena that are restricted to groups. For example, a single individual can never be characterized as dominant, but the concept *dominance* may usefully describe something about the social relationships within a group, including the positions of particular individuals within those relationships. Because groups of more than two present great technical difficulties to the analyst, most studies of group phenomena are restricted to observations of the interactions of two individuals (a dyad).

When investigating group social phenomena, the researcher is no longer interested in the individual behavior units per se. He or she is drawn instead to such things as the constellation of patterns exhibited by an animal, the context in which the animal operates, and the skill with which the animal engages in social behavior. These interests frequently lead to attempts to identify the various social roles within a group and to ascertain the degree to which they are occupied by particular individuals or by members of demographically defined groups (such as males, juveniles, or primiparas). Alternatively, social-behavior phenomena are treated as problems in motivation; much of the research on sexual or maternal behavior is clearly analogous, methodologically, to studies of hunger motivation.

All social behavior involves interaction between at least two individuals, by definition. However, sequence analysis of interactions can be applied effectively or legitimately only to behavior that is restricted to relatively brief time periods during which the nature of the relationship between the actors does not change. Because animals do change as a result of the social interactions in which they partake, the requirement that the actors not change, that their behavior maintain *stationarity*, is usually not met for lengthy interactions. To change a partner is, indeed, the point of much social behavior; the behavior of a courting male, for example, is in many species necessary to develop reproductive mood in the female. Nonstationary social interactions require special analytic techniques. Unfortunately, the techniques are as yet only poorly developed. This may help to account for the fact that the interactive nature of much social behavior is often overlooked, with the result that higher-order terms describing interaction may be treated as properties of the social behavior of individuals. This is a difficult and recurrent problem, which some ethologists have begun to deal with.

One useful approach is to take a critical look at some of the more familiar higher-order categories, with the aim of finding out how they are rooted in observables. After lengthy observations, Rowell (1966) impressionistically judged the relative dominance status of members of a small group of captive baboons. Her objective was to compare her rankings with quantitative data on observable behavioral patterns, so that the basis of her dominance judgments could be made explicit. Rowell first compiled data on a particular type of social interaction—the encounter. She divided encounters into two sorts: *approach-approach* and *approach-retreat*. In encounters of the first sort, one baboon would initiate a social exchange with another and would be met with a reciprocal or receptive response. In encounters of the second sort, the approached baboon would move away or otherwise avoid the social exchange. As might be expected, Rowell found that only approach-retreat encounters were useful in predicting her dominance rankings. Then, on the basis of facial expressions and other communication patterns, Rowell divided approaches into "friendly" and "aggressive" approaches. When she compared these data with her dominance rankings, Rowell found that aggressive approaches could not account for her judgments of dominance status; instead, the best prediction of dominance rating was the number of retreats, whether from aggressive or friendly encounters.

Although one "sees" a dominant baboon as somehow possessing dominance, this is a perceptual (conceptual?) illusion. Dominance in these animals is a property of social interaction. Rowell (1972) presents a good case for the argument that the mechanism for the phenomenon, on an individual level, is best sought in the more "submissive" animals of the group. These are the animals that were suffering most acutely from stress, as evidenced by their enlarged adrenal glands, frequent dysentery, and early death. Their generally debilitated condition led them to be overly cautious in social exchanges, even friendly ones. Interestingly, Rowell (1972) was unable to observe dominance hierarchies of any kind in the relatively unstressed, free-living baboons of the Ishasha region of Africa.

A related descriptive approach that holds great promise for application to human development is demonstrated readily by the work of Hinde and his colleagues on rhesus monkeys (summarized in Hinde, 1974). Mother–infant monkey dyads were observed longitudinally. One focus of analysis was on the physical contact between a mother and her infant. Logically, a contact may be initiated by either member of a pair and, likewise, may be terminated by either member. The observations showed that, early in the infant's development, the infant takes the initiative in breaking contacts more frequently than in initiating them; therefore, the mother is primarily responsible for the physical contact that is observed between the two. As development proceeds, the infant's role shifts, and the infant gradually becomes the one primarily responsible for contact, initiating relatively more and breaking relatively fewer contacts than the mother. Simultaneously with this change, the mother becomes more active in terminating contacts. These measures, along with several others, demonstrate clearly that the mother–infant relationship is dynamic, that it is the product of the active contributions of both members of the dyad, and that, with thorough description in objective terms, the contributions of the two members can, to a certain extent, be teased apart. Although descriptions can never allow firm conclusions about causes, these descriptions are extremely powerful in their clarification of problems for experimental analysis.

The Clarification of Concepts

There are many concepts used to characterize the course of human psychological development that cannot be defined or evaluated adequately by research on humans. We have already shown that the usefulness of such concepts as *innate, experience,* and *maturation,* associated with the nature/ nurture controversy, must be reevaluated in light of animal-behavior research. Unfortunately, in many studies of human psychological development, researchers have used these concepts as explanations of behavioral development. Studies of animal behavioral development have shown that, although the concept *innate* may be used to describe behaviors that are relatively stable during development, it may not be used as a substitute for an explanation of the stability. Moreover, the fact that a behavior is stable in development does not warrant the conclusion that the experiences of the individual are not contributing to the behavior's stability or that the behavior is genetically determined. The concepts of maturation and experience have also been used as separate explanations of behavioral development, even though animal-behavior studies show that they are irrevocably fused in development.

Attachment. The concept of attachment, as it is used to describe the social/emotional relationship of human infants to their mothers, must also be modified on the basis of animal-behavior studies. As Cairns (1972a) has noted, the concept of attachment has two separable meanings. In one sense, *attachment* describes the tendency of the infant, expressed during the first two years after birth, to prefer the company and ministrations of particular persons. The concept can also be used in this sense to describe the early social relations of many other species of mammals. In the second, explanatory sense, *attachment* refers to a unitary process that motivates, directs, and regulates the infant's social preference. There is no way of adequately evaluating the validity of this second meaning of attachment by studying humans. However, the study of the developing social preferences of other mammals reveals that a number of processes are responsible.

For relatively helpless nonhuman mammalian young, the mother provides part of the context within which the entire behavioral repertoire of the young animal is enacted. This is as true for behavior patterns that cannot readily be classified as social as for those that can. For example, when the ambient temperature falls above or below the range that is optimal, there is a disruption in the behavior of young mammals that are not yet capable of regulating their own body temperature through physiological means. The mother is an important source of heat for these animals, and the young may regulate their body temperature behaviorally by adjusting their position along a heat gradient that extends from the mother's body—in other words, adjust their proximity to her—in the same way that they would adjust themselves along a heat gradient created by a heat lamp (Rosenblatt, 1976). Further, the infant's behavior is important in structuring the behavior of the mother, including the behavior that she addresses toward her young. This structuring occurs in two rather different ways. The infant's behavior may have an immediate and direct effect on what the mother does; for example, ultrasonic cries from a mouse pup stimulate nest-building in its mother (Noirot, 1974). The infant's behavior also affects the mother's state, or internal condition. Stimulation emanating from rat pups that are living with their mothers maintains the mothers in the hormonal state appropriate to lactation (Grosvenor, Maiweg, & Mena, 1970) and in a behavioral state of readiness to address maternal responses to the young (Rosenblatt, 1970). We can agree with Cairns (1972a) that it would be both artificial and misleading to extract only some of the features from this developmental nexus, lump them together as a single thing, and label them *attachment*.

When *attachment* is used as a descriptive term, one is encouraged to focus attention only on certain aspects of the social experiences of the infant, in relative isolation from other experiences, and is deflected from attending to the interactive nature of social development. Therefore, examination of social development in nonhuman mammals might lead one to conclude that the concept of attachment, as presently used, obscures the recognition both that many factors contribute to the organization of social relations and that the mother–infant social relationship is a phase in a developmental sequence having important antecedents and consequences.

Aggression.   Similarly, Cairns (1972b) has argued that the concept of aggression has had the effect of delaying recognition of the diversity of factors contributing to the development of fighting behavior. Too often the concept of aggression has been used to refer to a characteristic of an individual rather than to the pattern of interaction between two individuals behaving within a specific situation and having particular developmental histories. It has been shown in mice that at least some of the observed sex differences in fighting behavior are explained by hormone-related odor differences. Androgen-dependent odors, such as are normally found in intact males, are potent stimuli for eliciting fighting from a second animal. Females and castrated males do not typically elicit many aggressive responses from companions and, therefore, do not engage in many fights. However, when urine from intact males is used to scent females and castrated males, these odorous animals elicit more aggressive behavior from others than they normally would (Lee & Griffo, 1973; Svare & Gandelman, 1974) and will, therefore, engage in more fighting. Recall from Rowell's (1966, 1972) work that dominance in baboons is an interactive phenomenon and that there is a surprisingly low correlation between aggression and dominance. Treating aggression as a characteristic that develops in and belongs to individuals is not only inappropriate; it will also hinder the discovery of the means whereby aggression may be regulated in humans.

Critical period.   The concept of *critical period*—a concept that belonged originally to embryology and that was introduced into the study of behavior by ethologists—has come into wide use in explanations of various aspects of the intellectual, social, and emotional development of humans (Connolly, 1972). The concept is difficult to evaluate when applied to humans, and experimental investigations have shown it to be misleading when applied to behavioral development of animals. Scott (1962) used the concept to describe features of the social development of such altricial mammals as kittens and puppies. The work of Schneirla and Rosenblatt (1963; Rosenblatt, 1976) has shown that no single age period can be singled out, however, as *the* period of importance for social development. Rather, each phase of development contributes to succeeding phases in ways that are crucial. The kitten begins to adjust to the mother at birth through use of the behavioral systems that it has available to it; as new systems emerge in development, the kitten makes new adjustments to the mother, based on the new systems and the experience gained through adjustments made during earlier phases.

By separating kittens from their mothers and keeping them on artificial brooders, Schneirla and Rosenblatt (1963) have shown that kittens that are separated from their mothers during various phases of social development have difficulty in adjusting to the mother on reunion. The artificial brooder has the effect of maintaining the kitten's social behavior at the developmental level achieved at the point of separation from the mother. The mother's social behavior continues to change during the separation period, however, because of her interaction with the remaining kittens. At reunion, the separated kitten behaves toward the mother in ways appropriate to an earlier phase of kitten–mother interaction, thereby producing discordant interactions between itself and the mother. All separated kittens manifest difficulties in their social adjustments, no matter when during development the separation occurs. It must be concluded that no single period during development is any more crucial for social development than any other. However, the particular difficulties in social adjustment that are manifested after separation depend on the level of social behavior achieved by the kitten before separation. The degree of difficulty at reunion will depend on the degree of discrepancy between the separated kitten's level of social behavior and that of its mother. Because the process of social development is continuous, to focus attention on the investigation of critical periods in social development actually can obscure the processes involved in the transitions from one level of social skill to another.

The notion of critical periods in social development also promotes a misleadingly sharp distinction between social and nonsocial processes. In rat pups, the nest plays an important mediating role in the development of behavior patterns that are later addressed to the mother and siblings. As soon as the pup is able to show oriented locomotion, which is at first a rather primitive crawl, it can get itself to the nest by following an odor gradient that terminates in the highly concentrated odor deposits found in the nest. The nest is also warmer than surrounding areas, creating a temperature gradient that is also followed by the pup. By its behavioral adjustments to odor and temperature, the young pup keeps itself in the nest, where, because of the mother's attraction to the nest and young, all interactions with the mother occur. The young pup responds to its mother and to its siblings in ways that are at least partially identical to its responses to the nest. All of the inhabitants of the nest share odor characteristics of the nest and therefore elicit approach responses. Because the mother and siblings are warmer than the nest, the pup will further adjust itself to maintain contact with them while in the nest (Rosenblatt, 1976). When the pup begins to walk in a coordinated fashion, it makes excursions from the nest. At this time, it can go directly to the mother by following the odor, or pheromone, that she emits only during the latter half of lactation (Leon & Moltz, 1971). The pup can therefore initiate contact with the mother—to suckle, for example—whether she is in the nest or not. When the eyes open, the use of visual cues becomes incorporated into the pup's social behavior, and social behavior continues its progressive reorganization.

Use of the critical-period concept focuses undue attention on the age of the individual at the expense of its developmental status. The concept also leads one to expect that, unless some particular sort of experience has occurred before the end of some specifiable time interval, a process of development can no longer be affected by experience. The individual will have missed the boat, so to speak. The use of the concept can, in other words, engender a feeling of hopelessness that can interfere with the proper work of developmentalists and that can have unfortunate practical consequences when applied to humans. Its use hardly has heuristic value; it is more likely to foreshorten developmental inquiry than to expand it. In view of these problems and of the failure of the concept to account adequately for social development of animals, the developmental psychologist interested in humans would be well advised to exercise skepticism when critical periods are postulated as important determinants of human developmental processes.

In conclusion, we would argue that animal-behavior studies can be important means of ferreting out misleading and invalid concepts of behavioral development. Such studies also allow concepts that are crucial to the description of human psychological development to be discerned. And this leads us to the next contribution of animal behavior to the understanding of human development.

The Identification of Special Features of Human Development

Comparison of human psychological development with animal behavioral development—particularly primate development—can reveal the unique and ubiquitous characteristics of human development. Knowledge of animal behavior can provide the investigator of human psychological development with another, broader perspective from which to examine the phenomena of human development. From this perspective, the researcher cannot help but be impressed by the extent to which language and reasoning skills influence and pervade the psychological development of humans. Even recent work with preverbal infants suggests that their social and sensory-motor development can best be characterized as a continual process of formulating and testing hypotheses about themselves and their sociophysical environments and elaborating rules of conduct (Kagan, 1971; Lewis & Lee-Painter, 1974; Richards, 1974).

Imitation.   In striking contrast to animals, children are able to imitate environmental as well as social events and are unflagging in their determination to do so. The ability to imitate combines with the child's interest in being taught and with the adult's propensity for direct tuition to generate a process of education that is found in all human cultures. The long period of dependency characteristic of human development makes this educational process possible, and the human species has capitalized on education as a means of maximizing developmental gains. During the protracted period of dependency, the individual not only receives a somewhat formalized education in the values and ways of his or her culture but also is presented with a variety of social roles to occupy and master. The complexity of these roles and of their interrelationship in even the simplest of human societies is well beyond that observed in animal social organization. As Schneirla (1966) argued, comparisons of human with animal behavioral development may be more instructive for the differences that are revealed than for the similarities that are discovered.

Play.   Consider the concept of play, which has often been used to describe certain phases of the social and sensory-motor development of animals (see Welker, 1971). Dolhinow and Bishop (1970) have argued that the social and solitary play of young primates is important for the development of the social and sensory-motor skills needed by adults to meet effectively the conditions of the environment and social structure of which they are a part. As important as these play patterns may be, they seem to be relatively confined to the preadult stages. It is seldom that sexually mature primates engage in social or solitary activities having no significant immediate consequences for survival. Yet, the adult human appears to do just that. Sensory-motor skills are elaborated beyond their functional necessity and are developed into art forms or formalized games. Once established as goals in themselves, they must be integrated into the social role structure. Even though the play of human and nonhuman primates shares some characteristics, play in humans is made unique through its incorporation into other, distinctively human activities.

In addition to formalizing sensory-motor skills into art forms and games, humans also create social-interaction routines from functional skills and elaborate them as social techniques for gaining and maintaining influence, power, fame, and control. Employment of these social routines extends beyond functional necessity and appears to involve little more than a wish to "play the game." Bruner (1972) may be quite right in insisting that play is a fundamental component of human social and intellectual development. However, it is only by contrast with the play of other animals that the unique, and possibly most significant, aspects of human play become obvious.

The Identification of Issues in Human Development That Need Study

Very often studies of animal behavior reveal factors affecting development that have been more or less ignored or considered unimportant by investigators of human development. In this way, animal studies stimulate and support research efforts in new domains of human development. We believe that there are at least five issues in human psychological development the study of which has been fostered or revitalized by animal-behavior research.

The influence of prenatal conditions on postnatal development.   In mammals, including humans, the mother and her offspring share a physiological intimacy from the moment of conception to birth. Normal development of the embryo is dependent upon the occurrence of many physiological events, regulated by the mother's neuroendocrine system. The evidence from animal-behavior studies demonstrates that socioenvironmental factors, which influence the mother's neuroendocrine condition, can have profound effects on the postnatal development of her offspring (Rosenblatt, 1967). Similarly, in human development, socioenvironmental factors, including those that produce stress, neuroses, psychoses, frustrations, and satisfactions, can affect the mother's neuroendocrine system, resulting in changed proportions of specific hormones. Many of these hormones pass the placental barrier and enter into the fetus's blood system, where they may eventually affect the developing fetal neuroendocrine system. Because the neuroendocrine system is responsible, in part, for an individual's reactivity to stimulation, its activity rhythms, and its ability to cope with situations and to organize behavioral responses (Levine, 1972), the neonate's behavior and course of development may show the consequences of socioenvironmental factors that affected the mother's physiology.

Birch (1972) has suggested that these socioenvironmental factors need not be present during the pregnancy to affect the development of offspring. Female rats that were malnourished when young, but not when adult or when pregnant, bore offspring that were smaller and behaviorally less competent than rats derived from normally nourished females. Third-generation young also showed the effects of their grandmother's malnourishment, even though they and their mothers had never been malnourished. Birch suggested that malnourishment early in a female rat's life disrupts her neuroendocrine physiology, with the result that later she provides a less-than-optimal intrauterine environment for her offspring. This changed intrauterine environment so affects the offspring that their intrauterine environments are also less than optimal, despite the fact that they have never been malnourished. Thus, a cross-generational socioenvironmental effect, mediated by neuroendocrine and intrauterine conditions, can be established.

Birch (1971) actually extended these findings to the analysis of a human-development issue. Hospital studies had indicated that the condition of the infant (birth weight, mortality, and morbidity) was more highly correlated with the race of the mother than with her socioeconomic status. These results were particularly perplexing because the birth condition of the infant ought to reflect the quality of prenatal nutrition and care received by the mother during pregnancy, and these factors were expected to vary according to the socioeconomic status of the mother rather than according to her race. Yet the condition of neonates born to middle-class Black mothers was not better than that of neonates born to lower-class White mothers. The condition of neonates born to middle-class White mothers, however, was significantly better than that of neonates born to either lower-class White or middle-class Black mothers.

Birch decided to divide the middle-class Black mothers into two groups: those born into middle-class circumstances and those born into lower-class circumstances. If lower-class circumstances result in poorer prenatal and postnatal nutrition and health care, then these factors may result in an intrauterine environment that is less than optimal for the next generation despite the good nutrition and health care available to the adult as part of her new, middle-class circumstances. Indeed, dividing the middle-class Black mothers into these two groups revealed the expected correlation of the infant's birth condition with the socioeconomic status of the mother. However, it was the socioeconomic status of the mother at the time of *her* birth, and not at the time of her pregnancy, that was relevant.

The fact that many animal-behavior studies have demonstrated the influence on the behavioral development of the young of socioenvironmental factors directly affecting the mother calls for an examination of the effects of such events on the psychological development of humans.

Parent–young reciprocity. The human being, like most mammals, is born into an intimate social setting involving one or more adults. The social contacts of the dependent mammalian infant contribute an enormous proportion of what might be called its *Umwelt,* or personal environment. Because this environment is social—that is, provided by other living individuals—it is not static. The caregivers and other social companions of infants are also undergoing development—sometimes as dramatic as that of the infant. Animal research has shown that the developmental changes in infants and their caregivers are interrelated (Rosenblatt, 1970; Schneirla, Rosenblatt, & Tobach, 1963); the behavioral development of young, therefore, is best characterized within the framework of parent–young reciprocity.

The effect of the changing characteristics of young on adults is illustrated nicely by the work of researchers who prevented maternal development in female rats by suspending development of their young (Wiesner & Sheard, 1933). Rats were allowed to give birth and rear their young for several days, whereupon the young were removed and replaced with younger, foster pups; the second litter was accepted and, in turn, replaced after several days. This procedure was repeated several times. The mother rats continued to show lactation and maternal behavior appropriate for young pups as long as the experimenters kept the pups young.

Rosenblatt (1965) has shown that the rat mother's behavior reflects a developing maternal condition and is not merely a series of responses to stimulation. When rats were allowed to live with their own developing young but were tested daily for responses to constant-age foster pups presented to them for brief periods, the rats showed developmental changes in their behavior that were apparent in their responses both to their own pups and to the constantly young foster pups. For example, the mothers failed to retrieve the young foster pups, normally highly effective in eliciting retrieval, shortly after retrieving had declined in the home litter situation. Maternal behavior is thus not simply a matter of selection of responses to match the stimulation from infants. Maternal behavior changes in a truly developmental fashion, and the young contribute actively to this process. The mothers in Wiesner and Sheard's (1933) study were, in essence, not allowed to undergo the developmental changes that would ordinarily have led to weaning, or termination of the mother–infant relationship.

The nature of parent–young interaction can also affect the course of infant development. Hinde and Spencer-Booth (1967) have shown that mother rhesus monkeys living in social groups are more likely to prevent the departure of their young from them and to retrieve them when they have departed than are rhesus mothers living alone with their infants. Consequently, weaning, or the attainment of independence as evidenced in willingness to spend more time exploring away from the mother, occurs both sooner and in a different fashion in the solitary dyads.

The nature of this reciprocal relationship between parent and offspring can be rather well-meshed and synchronous or disordered and disruptive. For example, Brazelton, Koslowski, & Main (1974) have observed that the behavioral interaction of human mothers and their infants during the first 4 to 20 weeks postpartum can be characterized as the establishment of a routine. The infant appears to go through cycles of "attention" and "inattention," during which it is either responsive, initiating social exchange, or unresponsive. Because of their sensitivity to their infants, mothers quickly adjust their interaction with the infant to coincide predominantly with the infant's "attention" phase. Presumably as a result of establishing this rhythm of social exchange, the infant gradually extends the duration of its attention phase, thereby providing for and engaging in longer and more complex social exchanges.

Sander (1970) has reported that the infant and its caregiver can have established reciprocal routines of interaction—albeit very simple ones—as early as 15 days postpartum. Klaus and Kennell (1970) have argued that normal hospital obstetrical routines may significantly interfere with the establishment of parent–offspring reciprocity, particularly in the case of infants restricted to incubators. If, as is usually the case, the mother is not allowed to care for her infant while it is in the incubator, a reciprocal social relationship is not established with the infant, and the development of the child can be adversely affected. Children whose mothers were allowed to care for them while they were restricted to incubators do not show these disruptions in psychological development (Ringler, Kennell, Jarvella, Navojosky, & Klaus, 1974).

Because of the reciprocal nature of the parent–young relationship, any effects that an event has on the development of young while they are still dependent on their parents may be due either to the direct effects of the event on the young or to the response of the parent to changed characteristics of the young. For example, animal studies of the effects of early experience showed that rats that were handled by humans during the first three weeks after birth were more exploratory and less "emotional" as adults, even when this handling was limited to a three-minute episode. At one time, it was presumed that this effect of early experience on the adult's behavior was a direct consequence of the handling. However, recent work calls this presumption into question. The behavior of mouse (Priestnall, 1973) and rat (Lee & Williams, 1974) mothers was observed after their young had undergone a typical handling procedure. In both species, mothers licked young pups that had been handled more than pups of comparable ages that had not received the treatment. It is therefore likely that the handling procedure exerts its long-term effect on the young at least partly by altering the nature of parent–infant interaction.

The consequences of the reciprocal nature of the parent–young relationship can extend beyond the boundaries of parental care. The primate literature, for instance, abounds in examples of mothers' acquiring new skills and habits through the observation of the self-acquired skills of their offspring (Hinde, 1974). Remember the transmission of the potato-washing skill of Japanese monkeys that was mentioned in Chapter Two.

Knowledge of the reciprocal nature of parent–young relationships in animals should stimulate more inquiry concerning the reciprocity of human parent–young relationships and its significance in human development. The animal studies should direct attention not only to the influence of the parents on the development of the young but also to effects of the young on the performance of the parent (see Bell, 1968, 1974). The results of these studies should stimulate attempts to describe precisely and characterize the reciprocity in the parent–young relationship (for example, Lewis & Lee-Painter, 1974) and its changes with time (for example, Sander, 1970). The results of animal-behavior research suggest that it is in the reciprocal relationships in which the child participates that the origins of its later psychological characteristics will be found.

The role of self-stimulation in development.   Schneirla (1957) has argued that "the individual seems to be interactive with itself throughout development" (p. 86). At each stage of development, the organism exhibits specific behavioral abilities in interaction with its social and physical environment. The application of these behavioral abilities provides the individual with certain specific kinds of stimulation from the environment, which become, in turn, experiences that influence the individual's development. These "circular relationships of self-stimulation" (p. 86) are an important source of behavioral development. We have already shown, in Chapter Three, that the prehatching peeping of the embryonic duck provides it with the auditory experience responsible for the organization of its posthatching responsiveness to the maternal call (Gottlieb, 1975). Also, Held and Hein (1963) experimentally demonstrated that the visual stimulation provided by the kitten's own locomotion is responsible for the development of certain important visual-motor perceptual abilities. Eye–paw coordination, for example, develops appropriately in kittens that can simultaneously walk and look at things but not in kittens that can look at things only while passively being moved.

Just as self-produced stimulation is important for kitten perceptual-motor development, it also appears to be important for sensory-motor development of human infants (Piaget, 1953). It is a result of feeling and seeing changes in the positions of their limbs in relation to one another, to the body, and to objects in the environment that infants develop coordinated sensory-motor skills and abilities. Piaget called instances of this kind of self-stimulation *circular reactions* and considered them a major source for the intellectual development of the human infant.

The individual's contribution to the experiences influencing his or her development has been pretty much ignored in theories and studies of human psychological development. The results of animal-behavior studies suggest that a closer examination of the role of self-induced stimulation in human psychological development is warranted.

The role of nonadult companions in development.   Recent research has drawn attention to the importance of nonadult companions in the behavioral development of young monkeys and apes (Harlow & Harlow, 1965; Hinde, 1974). Again, this social influence is characterized by reciprocity; interaction among age-mates stimulates development in all parties. When there is an age disparity in the relationship, developmental changes are induced in older individuals as a consequence of their interactions with younger ones, and vice versa. Peers, and not adults, appear to have the most influence on the social and emotional development of the young nonhuman primate (Dolhinow & Bishop, 1970).

Interestingly, Piaget (1948) has suggested that interaction with nonadult companions is an important influence in an individual's cognitive development, as well. Murray (1972) and Turiel (1969) have demonstrated that the conflicts experienced by a child when his or her interpretation and explanation of events are at variance with those of cognitively more mature companions stimulate rapid cognitive development.

Although the role of nonadult companions in human psychological development could be of major significance for the handling of child-rearing, education, and therapy, it has received little systematic investigation.

The continuance of developmental processes throughout the life span.   Once an animal has become sexually mature or adult, its behavioral development does not come to an end, nor are questions about its development inappropriate. Many animals engage in several reproductive cycles, exhibiting demonstrable changes from one cycle to the next (Lehrman, 1961). Even short-lived animals that exhibit only one reproductive experience before dying typically engage in a reproductive cycle consisting of phases of behavioral changes reminiscent of developmental phenomena. Finally, the transformation of an individual from one that is capable of reproduction to one incapable of reproduction is also a developmental event, influenced by both the immediate and remote experiences of the animal.

In certain primates and other animals that exhibit rather complex social organizations, an individual may engage in a number of role changes, requiring different behaviors, during the course of its life that are somewhat independent of its reproductive status.

All of these phenomena point to the need to study human psychological development beyond the boundaries of the individual's initiation into adult society. Changes in the adult's psychological characteristics are both consequences of antecedent events in his or her history and prerequisites for later-occurring abilities. Human psychological development is as much a life-span phenomenon as animal behavioral development is.

Some Recent Attempts at Synthesis

Two recent attempts to establish a relationship between animal-behavior studies and human development have generated a measure of popular interest and some professional discussion. These attempts at synthesis are called *human ethology* and *sociobiology*. A proper appraisal of the significant contributions of either would require a presentation beyond the scope of this book. Nevertheless, we would be remiss if we did not present, at least briefly, some introduction to their positions. We suggest that you augment this discussion with a review of Chapters Two and Three of this book.

Human Ethology

Human ethology is a label covering a loose conglomerate of research activities that have blossomed during the last decade. These have included: misguided attempts to apply the theories and constructs of classical ethology to the study of human behavior; fruitless searches for the natural behaviors of humans; identification of human behaviors that are similar in their patterning and social consequences across all cultures; and sophisticated descriptions of behavior in typical human settings. Much of the human ethological research represents an attempt to describe behaviors presumed to have survival value for the human species.

Classical ethological theory has suffered total rejection of many of its features and major revision of the rest of them. There is no generally accepted theory or set of constructs that can be said to define ethology today. Therefore, any attempt to carve out a new discipline of human ethology by applying the remnants of classical ethological theory to human behavior is doomed from the beginning. The several attempts to do so (for example, Lorenz, 1966; Morris, 1967) have excited the popular and scientific imagination and may continue to do so for a while. They cannot provide a firm foundation for the reorganization of the approach to human behavior, however—for three reasons. The first has already been mentioned: the theory is in trouble on its home ground. Second, their methodological approach to human behavior is blantantly anecdotal. The armchair approach to human behavior was thrown out by psychology in the last century, and with good reason. There is absolutely no reason to restore it. Finally, the ethologists who have engaged in this enterprise have violated one of their own principles, defended as sacred when animals are the objects of study. The principle is that each species must be studied as a separate entity having unique properties. When humans are studied by analogy with some other species, be it coral-reef fishes or chimpanzees, they are not being studied ethologically—that is, as humans.

Others have focused on the field, or naturalistic/descriptive, approach, often equated with the ethological method, as the definitive basis for creating a human ethology. The argument that human ethologists must be concerned with behavior that occurs naturally in the field sets enormous problems. What is natural human behavior? It certainly cannot be defined, as it is in animals, as free from human interference. And what is a field situation, for humans? A nursery school or a street corner may be "field-like," in the sense that they were not designed for the purposes of studying behavior, but, like laboratories, they are human contrivances, and they do structure behavior. In sum, it is much easier to distinguish between natural and unnatural behavior and between natural and unnatural settings when another species is at issue; at least, it is much easier for us to be happy with the distinctions.

The difficulty in making these distinctions for human behavior in our own society has led some investigators to search for primordial human behavior and primordial human environments among hunter/gatherer cultures —cultures believed to resemble those of early humans (Bowlby, 1969). This practice raises questions of its own, but, in addition, it does not really speak to the question of behavior in our society and our time. Ethologists who study human behavior or psychologists who wish to adopt naturalistic methods will have to resign themselves to the fact that there is no ready means for making a clear distinction between natural and artificial human environments.

Provided that the investigator does not become too concerned with the search for natural human conditions, careful and detailed observations of human behavior under relatively free conditions (that is, conditions that allow the individual several options concerning what to do) can be of enormous value in suggesting useful hypotheses or avenues for further investigation. We have discussed the important and constructive role that sophisticated observational methods, in the hands of human ethologists such as Blurton Jones and Richards, have played in the reformulation of thinking about human mother–infant relationships.

Other human ethologists (for example, Eibl-Eibesfeldt, 1975) have turned their attention to a search for universal, or species-specific, human behavior patterns—a search that is carried out through cross-cultural comparisons. Their findings are informative and interesting and set problems for developmental psychologists. They do not, as is sometimes claimed, settle developmental questions by distinguishing between learned and innate behavior. The discovery that a behavior pattern is species-universal tells nothing about its development.

It seems to us that it would be unwise for human ethologists to construct a narrowly defined, separate discipline. It would also be both unwise and absurd to exclude the human animal from ethology's purview. The wisest choice, it seems, would be to define both ethology and psychology in the broadest possible terms so that interdisciplinary exchange can occur. It would be foolish for ethologists to discard the breadth they have brought to the study of animal behavior when they turn their attention to humans. It is exactly that breadth that would make the greatest contribution to psychology. It would be equally foolish to ignore all that psychologists have learned about human behavior (see Bernal & Richards, 1973; Blurton Jones, 1974).

Sociobiology

The second attempt to synthesize the study of animal behavior with human psychology involves the extension of the constructs and theories of the "new" biological discipline, currently called *sociobiology*, to the social psychology of humans (Wilson, 1975). Such human-development issues as sex-role acquisition, child-care activities, moral development, preference for sexual partners, and the socialization of ethnic and racial attitudes are interpreted within the framework of certain theories of evolution, ecology, and population biology.

Field studies over the past century have revealed the vast diversity of animal social organizations. Some species exhibit organizations consisting of large numbers of animals with well-defined roles. Other species exhibit similar organizations but only at certain times of the year or in certain environmental circumstances. Many species exhibit organizations of large numbers of individuals but only a few, if any, roles. In many species, individuals are solitary, sometimes even to the point of not coming together during sexual reproduction. In others, members select mates for life and then either remain continuously with them or seek them during the breeding season. Some species have social organizations consisting of a single male and his harem and offspring. Others consist of large numbers of females and their offspring, with males venturing to enter the group only during the breeding season and then only at great risk. The list continues.

What is most striking about this diversity of animal social organization is that the complexity of social organization (but not necessarily the mechanisms used to achieve the organization) is independent of phylogenetic history. Complex social organizations are not restricted to species of more recently evolved populations. Rather, certain species of crustacea, insects, fish, birds, and mammals, including some primates, exhibit similarly complex social organizations. Examination of the similarities of social organization across phylogenetically distant species and the dissimilarities among phylogenetically close species has revealed that social organization is closely associated with ecological conditions. Species facing similar ecological circumstances exhibit similar social organization.

The strength of sociobiology lies in its ability to interpret and partially to predict a species's social organization from information about a rather limited set of ecological conditions. These conditions include the type of food the species utilizes and the stability and predictability of the food's occurrence; the dispersal pattern, in time and space, of food, shelter, and other resources the species uses; the activities of the species's predators and parasites; and the rapidity of change in the environment. These and other ecological conditions restrict the range of social organizations that would be adaptive in any given environment.

The significance of sociobiology lies in its recognition that a group's social structure is often a solution to a specific set of problems posed by its environment. Unfortunately, in theorizing about the relationship between the environment and animal behavior, sociobiologists have too often relied on some unwarranted assumptions, and this has tended to interfere with the acceptance of their position.

Consider the phenomenon of child care. The first question posed by the sociobiologist would be "Why do humans care for their offspring?" Given the abilities of the infant and child and the conditions of the environment, it can easily be assumed that parental care is necessary for the survival of the offspring. Therefore, there is a strong natural selection favoring child care. The sociobiologist may assume further that the basic characteristics of the care are genetically determined.

But why is it often the biological parent who provides the care, and not just any adult? Sociobiologists assume that each individual attempts to maximize the representation of his or her particular genes in the gene pool of the population. This is achieved by reproduction. The more of one's offspring in a population, the more representation of one's genes in the gene pool. Parental care ensures the survival of the offspring and therefore their occurrence in the population. However, parental care involves some investment of energy and time on the part of the caregiver. Sociobiologists further assume that there is both a level of care necessary to ensure the survival of the young and a limit to the amount of care that can be provided before it becomes destructive to the caregiver. The degree to which an individual will invest resources in caregiving will be related to the degree of genetic similarity between the caregiver and caretaker. Because the biological parent is likely to have more genes in common with its offspring than any other individual in the population, parental care will be associated with the biological parent. Genes of individuals who invest energy in the care of genetically unrelated offspring will quickly disappear from the gene pool after several generations.

If parental care is so good, why does weaning occur? Offspring typically possess only a portion of their genes in common with a parent; no parent and offspring are genetically identical. The offspring, therefore, will also be trying to maximize *their* contribution to the gene pool. The more parental care they receive, the better their chances of survival. However, the more parental care an individual provides, the less his or her chance of survival and/or of producing more offspring. The interactions between parent and offspring will reflect a conflict of genetic interest, with offspring trying to maintain or increase parental care and with parents trying to reduce it. The point at which further parental investment would become detrimental to the parents' contribution to the gene pool marks the beginning of the weaning process. Thus, the sociobiologist might argue that there can never be a trauma-free weaning.

In evaluating the sociobiological explanation, you must recognize that it is an interpretation of already-known information and not a prediction about events not yet observed. As such, it provides a new perspective (in addition to the psychoanalytic, developmental psychobiological, social-learning, and other perspectives) from which to view the child care of humans. Any fault in the sociobiological perspective would lie in an overly enthusiastic assumption that it is the only "true" perspective.

The sociobiological position leads to the posing of questions and seeking of answers about the function and phylogeny of behavior, not about its causation and development. In order to make plausible functional and phylogenetic interpretations, the sociobiologist must often assume that the development of behavior is a simple reflection of maturation of the nervous system as determined by genes. Obviously, this is an assumption that a developmental psychobiologist cannot accept; nor is such an assumption warranted by the study of social organization and ecology.

Evidence consistently demonstrates that the social organization of many species will change dramatically with shifts in their ecological conditions (Emlen, 1976). The assumption of genetic determination of behavioral development is not only inappropriate but also irrelevant to the sociobiological position. That behavior is not genetically determined does not detract from the importance of recognizing that it is adapted to particular ecological demands or that there may be few behavioral solutions to certain ecological problems.

In applying sociobiological principles to human societies, one must either ignore or deemphasize many of the unique features of these societies. For example, many cultures have managed to exploit the resources of the ecology with technological and social strategies that act as partial buffers between the ecological conditions and the society. Thus, populations can increase beyond the carrying capacity of the immediate ecology, and ecologically maladaptive societal activities can be undertaken. Human beings, with their ability to conceive of their ecological resources as worldwide and virtually infinitely augmentable by technological and managerial means, can achieve a complexity of social organization unlike that of any other animal species and independent of the forces considered by any current sociobiological positions.

The sociobiological position alerts us to the importance of attending to the ecological limitations on the exploitation of natural resources by any societal organization. It calls on people to seriously consider adjustment of their societies to a more "conservationist" relationship with the ecosystems of the planet. However, as a means for explaining or interpreting human societies and their characteristics, sociobiology is nothing more than provocative speculation.

Summary

In this chapter we have tried to show that the natural-history orientation to the study of animal behavior can provide an enriching outlook on human psychological development. Attention to natural-history-oriented studies provides the investigator of human development with a vantage point from which to discover the species-typical characteristics of human psychology. Animal-behavior studies can provide support for studies of human psychological development that do not fit the current mold of human-research efforts. Yet, although the ideas, issues, techniques, and approaches that accompany the study of behavioral development of animals may be applicable to studies of human development, the data, theories, and explanatory constructs of animal-behavior studies are not applicable.

Finally, in this chapter we have sought to demonstrate that there is much to gain from the integration of biology and psychology and from the adoption of the developmental-psychobiological approach to human development. This approach provides yet another perspective from which to view the psychological development of that most perplexing animal facing us in our mirrors every morning.

References

Ambrose, J. A. The comparative approach to early child development: The data of ethology. In E. Miller (Ed.), *Foundations of child psychiatry*. Oxford: Pergamon Press, 1968.

Anderson, J. W. Attachment behaviour out of doors. In N. Blurton Jones (Ed.), *Ethological studies of child behaviour*. London: Cambridge University Press, 1972.

Anderson, P. W. More is different. *Science*, 1972, *177*, 393–396.

Ardrey, R. *The territorial imperative: A personal inquiry into the animal origins of property and nations*. New York: Atheneum Press, 1966.

Aries, P. *Centuries of childhood*. New York: Knopf, 1962.

Atz, J. W. The application of the idea of homology to behavior. In L. R. Aronson, E. Tobach, D. S. Lehrman, & J. S. Rosenblatt (Eds.), *Development and evolution of behavior*. San Francisco: Freeman, 1970.

Ayala, F. J., & Dobzhansky, T. *Studies in the philosophy of biology: Reduction and related problems*. Berkeley: University of California Press, 1974.

Bakeman, R. *Some approaches to the analysis of mother-infant interaction*. Paper presented at the Biennial Meeting of the Society for Research in Child Development, Denver, April 10, 1975.

Barlow, H. B., & Pettigrew, J. D. Lack of specificity of neurones in the visual cortex of young kittens. *Journal of Physiology*, (London), 1971, *218*, 98–100.

Bateson, P. P. G. The characteristics and context of imprinting. *Biological Reviews*, 1966, *41*, 177–220.

Bateson, P. P. G. The imprinting of birds. In S. A. Barnett (Ed.), *Ethology and development*. Philadelphia: Lippincott, 1973.

Beach, F. A. *Hormones and behavior*. New York: Harper & Row, 1948.

Beer, C. G. Species-typical behavior and ethology. In D. A. Dewsbury & D. A. Rethlingshafer (Eds.), *Comparative psychology: A modern survey*. New York: McGraw-Hill, 1973.

Bell, R. Q. A reinterpretation of the direction of effects in studies of socialization. *Psychological Review*, 1968, *75*, 81–85.

Bell, R. Q. Contributions of human infants to caregiving and social interaction. In M. Lewis & L. A. Rosenbaum (Eds.), *The effect of the infant on its caregiver*. New York: Wiley, 1974.

Bernal, J. F., & Richards, M. P. M. What can zoologists tell us about human development? In S. A. Barnett (Ed.), *Ethology and development*. Philadelphia: Lippincott, 1973.

Bijou, S. W., & Baer, D. M. *Child development: A systematic and empirical theory* (Vol. 1). New York: Appleton-Century-Crofts, 1961.

Birch, H. G. Levels, categories, and methodological assumptions in the study of behavioral development. In E. Tobach, L. R. Aronson, & E. Shaw (Eds.), *The biopsychology of development.* New York: Academic Press, 1971.

Birch, H. G. Malnutrition, learning, and intelligence. *American Journal of Public Health,* 1972, *62,* 773–784.

Blakemore, C. Environmental constraints on development in the visual system. In R. A. Hinde & J. Stevenson-Hinde (Eds.), *Constraints on learning.* London and New York: Academic Press, 1973.

Blakemore, C. Development of the mammalian visual system. *British Medical Bulletin,* 1974, *30,* 152–157.

Blakemore, C., & Cooper, G. F. Development of the brain depends on the visual environment. *Nature,* 1970, *228,* 477–478.

Blurton Jones, N. G. Ethology and early socialization. In M. P. M. Richards (Ed.), *The integration of a child into a social world.* London: Cambridge University Press, 1974.

Blurton Jones, N., & Leach, G. M. Behaviour of children and their mothers at separation and greeting. In N. Blurton Jones (Ed.), *Ethological studies of child behaviour.* London: Cambridge University Press, 1972.

Bodmer, W. F., & Cavalli-Sforza, L. L. Intelligence and race. *Scientific American,* 1970, *223,* 19–29.

Bowlby, J. *Attachment and loss* (Vol. 1): *Attachment.* New York: Basic Books, 1969.

Brazelton, T. B., Koslowski, B., & Main, M. The origins of reciprocity: The early mother-infant interaction. In M. Lewis & R. A. Rosenblum (Eds.), *The effect of the infant on its caregiver.* New York: Wiley, 1974.

Bronfenbrenner, U. Is 80% of intelligence genetically determined? In U. Bronfenbrenner (Ed.), *Influences on human development.* Hinsdale, Ill.: Dryden, 1972.

Bronowski, J. *The ascent of man.* Boston: Little, Brown, 1973.

Bruner, J. S. Nature and uses of immaturity. *American Psychologist,* 1972, *27,* 687–708.

Cairns, R. B. Attachment and dependency: A psychobiological and social-learning synthesis. In J. L. Gewirtz (Ed.), *Attachment and dependency.* New York: Wiley, 1972. (a)

Cairns, R. B. Ontogenetic contributions to aggressive behavior. In F. J. Monks, W. W. Hartup, & J. deWit (Eds.), *Determinants of behavioral development.* New York: Academic Press, 1972. (b)

Carlson, E. A. *The gene: A critical history.* Philadelphia: Saunders, 1966.

Cavalli-Sforza, L. L., & Bodmer, W. F. *The genetics of human populations.* San Francisco: Freeman, 1971.

Cohen, J. J. A comparison of invertebrate and vertebrate central neurons. In F. O. Schmitt (Ed.), *The neurosciences: Second study program.* New York: Rockefeller University Press, 1970.

Connolly, K. Learning and the concept of critical periods in infancy. *Developmental Medicine and Child Neurology,* 1972, *14,* 705–714.

Crick, F. *Molecules and men.* Seattle: University of Washington Press, 1966.

Cullen, E. Adaptations in the kittiwake to cliff-nesting. *Ibis,* 1957, *99,* 275–302.

de Beer, G. R. *Embryos and ancestors* (3rd ed.). London: Oxford University Press, 1958.

DeFries, J. C., Thomas, E. A., Hegmann, J. P., & Weir, M. W. Open-field behaviour in mice: Analysis of maternal effects by means of ovarian transplantation. *Psychonomic Science,* 1967, *8,* 207–208.

DeFries, J. C., Weir, M. W., & Hegmann, J. P. Differential effects of prenatal maternal stress on offspring behavior in mice as a function of genotype and stress. *Journal of Comparative and Physiological Psychology*, 1967, *63*, 332–334.

Dingle, H. A statistical and information analysis of aggressive communication in the mantis shrimp *Gonodactylus bredini* Manning. *Animal Behaviour*, 1969, *17*, 561–575.

Dobzhansky, T. Of flies and men. *American Psychologist*, 1967, *22*, 41–48.

Dolhinow, P. J., & Bishop, N. The development of motor skills and social relationships among primates through play. In J. P. Hill (Ed.), *Minnesota symposia in child psychology* (Vol. 4). Minneapolis: University of Minnesota Press, 1970.

Eibl-Eibesfeldt, I. *Ethology* (2nd ed.). New York: Holt, Rinehart and Winston, 1975.

Emlen, S. T. An alternative case for sociobiology. *Science*, 1976, *192*, 736.

Freedman, D. G. A biological approach to personality development. In S. Washburn (Ed.), *Perspectives in human evolution I*. New York: Holt, Rinehart and Winston, 1968.

Gerall, A. A. An exploratory study of the effect of social isolation variables on the sexual behaviour of male guinea pigs. *Animal Behaviour*, 1963, *11*, 274–282.

Geschwind, N. The organization of language and the brain. *Science*, 1970, *170*, 940–944.

Ginsburg, B. E. Developmental behavioral genetics. In N. B. Talbot, J. Kagan, & L. Eisenberg (Eds.) *Behavioral science in pediatric medicine*. Philadelphia: Saunders, 1971.

Gottlieb, G. *Development of species identification in birds*. Chicago: University of Chicago Press, 1971.

Gottlieb, G. Development of species identification in ducklings. II. Experiential prevention of perceptual deficit caused by embryonic auditory deprivation. *Journal of Comparative and Physiological Psychology*, 1975, *89*, 675–684.

Grosvenor, C. E., Maiweg, H., & Mena, F. A study of factors involved in the development of the exteroceptive release of prolactin in the lactating rat. *Hormones and Behavior*, 1970, *1*, 111–120.

Gruber, H. E. Factors controlling the rate of conceptual change: A study of Charles Darwin's thinking. In *Concept formation and mental activity*. Symposium presented at 18th International Congress of Psychology, Moscow, August 1966.

Gruber, H. E., & Barrett, P. H. *Darwin on man: A psychological study of scientific creativity*. New York: Dutton, 1974.

Hambley, J. Diversity: A developmental perspective. In K. Richardson & D. Spears (Eds.), *Race and intelligence*. Baltimore: Penguin Books, 1972.

Hampson, J. L., & Hampson, J. G. The ontogenesis of sexual behavior in man. In W. C. Young (Ed.), *Sex and internal secretions* (Vol. 2, 3rd ed.). Baltimore: Williams & Wilkins, 1961.

Handler, P. *Biology and the future of man*. New York: Oxford University Press, 1970.

Harlow, H. F., & Harlow, M. K. The affectional systems. In A. M. Schrier, H. F. Harlow, F. Stollnitz (Eds.), *Behavior of nonhuman primates* (Vol. 2). New York and London: Academic Press, 1965.

Harris, G. W. *Neural control of the pituitary gland*. London: Arnold, 1955.

Held, R., & Hein, A. Movement-produced stimulation in the development of visually guided behavior. *Journal of Comparative and Physiological Psychology*, 1963, *56*, 872–876.

Hershenson, M. The development of visual perceptual systems. In H. Moltz (Ed.), *The ontogeny of vertebrate behavior*. New York: Academic Press, 1971.

Hinde, R. A. Development of social behavior. In A. M. Schrier & F. Stollnitz (Eds.), *Behavior of nonhuman primates* (Vol. 3). New York: Academic Press, 1971.

Hinde, R. A. *Biological bases of human social behavior*. New York: McGraw-Hill, 1974.

Hinde, R. A., & Spencer-Booth, Y. The effect of social companions on mother-infant relations in rhesus monkeys. In D. Morris (Ed.), *Primate Ethology*. New York: Anchor, 1967.

Hinde, R. A., & Stevenson-Hinde, J. (Eds.). *Constraints on learning*. New York: Academic Press, 1973.

Hirsch, J. Behavior-genetic analysis and its biosocial consequences. *Seminars in Psychiatry*, 1970, *2*, 89–105.

Hodos, W., & Campbell, C. B. G. *Scala naturae:* Why there is no theory in comparative psychology. *Psychological Review*, 1969, *76*, 337–350.

Horn, G., Stechler, G., & Hill, R. M. Receptive fields of units in the visual cortex of the cat in the presence and absence of bodily tilt. *Experimental Brain Research*, 1972, *15*, 113–132.

Hubel, D. H., & Wiesel, T. N. Receptive fields, binocular interaction and functional architecture in the cat's visual cortex. *Journal of Physiology*, 1962, *160*, 106–154.

Hull, D. L. Reduction in genetics-biology or philosophy? *Philosophy of Science*, 1972, *39*, 491–499.

Hutt, C. *Males and females*. Middlesex, England: Penguin Books, 1972.

Impekoven, M., & Gold, P. S. Prenatal origins of parent-young interactions in birds: A naturalistic approach. In G. Gottlieb (Ed.), *Behavioral embryology I*. New York: Academic Press, 1973.

Irvine, W. *Apes, angels and Victorians*. London: Readers Union, 1956.

Jacob, F., & Monod, J. Genetic regulatory mechanisms in the synthesis of proteins. *Journal of Molecular Biology*, 1961, *3*, 318–350.

Jaynes, J. The historical origins of "ethology" and "comparative psychology." *Animal Behaviour*, 1969, *17*, 601–606.

Jensen, A. R. How much can we boost IQ and scholastic achievement? *Harvard Educational Review*, 1969, *39*, 1–123.

Kagan, J. Personality development. In N. B. Talbot, J. Kagan, & L. Eisenberg (Eds.), *Behavioral science in pediatric medicine*. Philadelphia: Saunders, 1971.

Kamin, L. J. *The science and politics of IQ*. Potomac, Md.: Lawrence Erlbaum, 1974.

Kaplan, A. *The conduct of inquiry*. San Francisco: Chandler, 1964.

Kaufman, I. C. Mother/infant relations in monkeys and humans. In N. F. White (Ed.), *Ethology and psychiatry*. Toronto: University of Toronto Press, 1974.

Klaus, M. H., & Kennell, J. H. Mothers separated from their newborn infants. *Pediatric Clinics of North America*, 1970, *17*, 1015.

Klein, D. B. *A history of scientific psychology*. New York: Basic Books, 1970.

Klopfer, P. H. Evolution and behavior. In G. Bermant (Ed.), *Perspectives on animal behavior*. Glenview, Ill.: Scott, Foresman, 1973.

Kummer, H. *Primate societies*. New York: Aldine, 1971.

Lack, D. *Darwin's finches*. London: Cambridge University Press, 1947.

Lee, C. T., & Griffo, W. Early androgenization and aggression pheromone in inbred mice. *Hormones and Behavior*, 1973, *4*, 181–189.

Lee, M. H. S., & Williams, D. I. Changes in licking behaviour of rat mother following handling of young. *Animal Behaviour*, 1974, *22*, 679–681.

Lehrman, D. S. A critique of Konrad Lorenz's theory of instinctive behavior, *Quarterly Review of Biology*, 1953, *28*, 337–363.

Lehrman, D. S. Hormonal regulation of parental behavior in birds and infrahuman mammals. In W. C. Young (Ed.), *Sex and internal secretions* (3rd ed.). Baltimore: Williams & Wilkins, 1961.

Lehrman, D. S. Interaction of hormonal and experiential influences on the development of behavior. In E. L. Bliss (Ed.), *Roots of behavior*. New York: Harper, 1962.

Lehrman, D. S. The reproductive behavior of ring doves. *Scientific American*, 1964, *211*, 48–54.

Lehrman, D. S. Interaction between internal and external environments in the regulation of the reproductive cycle of the ring dove. In F. A. Beach (Ed.), *Sex and behavior*. New York: Wiley, 1965.

Lehrman, D. S. Semantic and conceptual issues in the nature-nurture problem. In L. R. Aronson, E. Tobach, D. S. Lehrman, & J. S. Rosenblatt (Eds.), *Development and evolution of behavior*. San Francisco: Freeman, 1970.

Lehrman, D. S. Behavioral science, engineering, and poetry. In E. Tobach, L. R. Aronson, & E. Shaw (Eds.), *The biopsychology of development*. New York: Academic Press, 1971.

Lehrman, D. S. Can psychiatrists use ethology? In N. F. White (Ed.), *Ethology and psychiatry*. Toronto: University of Toronto Press, 1974.

Leon, M., & Moltz, H. Maternal pheromone: Discrimination by pre-weanling Albino rats. *Physiology and Behavior*, 1971, *7*, 265–267.

Lerner, R. M. *Concepts and theories of human development*. Reading, Ma.: Addison Wesley, 1976.

Levine, S. Infantile stimulation: perspective. In A. Ambrose (Ed.), *Stimulation in early infancy*. New York: Academic Press, 1969.

Levine, S. (Ed.). *Hormones and behavior*. New York: Academic Press, 1972.

Lewis, M., & Lee-Painter, S. An interactional approach to the mother-infant dyad. In M. Lewis & L. A. Rosenblum (Eds.), *The effect of the infant on its caregiver*. New York: Wiley, 1974.

Lorenz, K. [The conception of instinctive behavior.] In C. H. Schiller (Ed. and trans.), *Instinctive behavior*. New York: International Universities Press, 1957. (Originally published 1937.)

Lorenz, K. *Evolution and modification of behaviour*. Chicago: University of Chicago Press, 1965.

Lorenz, K. *On Aggression*. New York: Harcourt Brace Jovanovich, 1966.

Lorenz, K. [Comparative studies of the motor patterns of Anatinae] (R. Martin, trans.). In K. Lorenz, *Studies in animal and human behaviour II*. Cambridge, Ma.: Harvard University Press, 1971. (Originally published 1941.) (a)

Lorenz, K. *Studies in animal and human behaviour II*. Cambridge, Ma.: Harvard University Press, 1971. (b)

Lytton, H., & Zwirner, W. Compliance and its controlling stimuli observed in a natural setting. *Developmental Psychology*, 1975, *11*, 769–779.

Maier, N. R. F., & Schneirla, T. C. *Principles of animal psychology*. New York: McGraw-Hill, 1935.

Marler, P., & Hamilton, W. J. III. *Mechanisms of animal behavior*. New York: Wiley, 1966.

Marshall, F. H. A. Sexual periodicity and the causes which determine it. *Philosophical Transactions*, 1936, *226B*, 423–456.

Mayr, E. *Animal species and evolution*. Cambridge, Ma.: Harvard University Press, 1963.

Mayr, E. Footnotes on the philosophy of biology. *Philosophy of Science*, 1969, *36*, 197–202.

McDougall, W. *An introduction to social psychology.* Kennebunkport, Maine: Milford House, 1973. (Originally published 1926.)

Mead, M. *Coming of age in Samoa.* New York: William Morrow, 1928.

Miller, N. E. Learning of visceral and glandular responses. *Science,* 1969, *163,* 434–445.

Miyadi, D. Social life of Japanese monkeys. *Science,* 1964, *143,* 783–786.

Moltz, H. Contemporary instinct theory and the fixed action pattern. *Psychological Review,* 1965, *72,* 27–47.

Moltz, H., & Stettner, L. J. The influence of patterned light deprivation on the critical period for imprinting. *Journal of Comparative and Physiological Psychology,* 1961, *54,* 279–283.

Money, J., & Ehrhardt, A. A. *Man and woman boy and girl.* Baltimore: Johns Hopkins University Press, 1972.

Moore, C. L. A psychobiological view of sexual differentiation. Paper in preparation, 1977.

Moore, D. J., & Shiek, D. A. Toward a theory of early infantile autism. *Psychological Review,* 1971, *78,* 451–456.

Morris, D. *The naked ape.* New York: McGraw-Hill, 1967.

Murray, F. Acquisition of conservation through social interaction. *Developmental Psychology,* 1972, *6,* 1–6.

Nelson, G. J. Outline of a theory of comparative biology. *Systematic Zoology,* 1970, *19,* 373–384.

Noirot, E. Nest-building by the virgin female mouse exposed to ultrasound from inaccessible pups. *Animal Behaviour,* 1974, *22,* 410–420.

Piaget, J. *The moral judgment of the child.* Glencoe, Ill.: Free Press, 1948.

Piaget, J. *The origins of intelligence.* New York: Basic Books, 1953.

Pittendrigh, C. S. Adaptation, natural selection, and behavior. In A. Roe & G. G. Simpson (Eds.), *Behavior and evolution.* New Haven, Conn.: Yale University Press, 1958.

Priestnall, R. Effects of handling on maternal behaviour in the mouse *(Mus musculus):* An observational study. *Animal Behaviour,* 1973, *21,* 383–386.

Ressler, R. H. Parental handling in two strains of mice reared by foster parents. *Science,* 1962, *137,* 129–130.

Ressler, R. H. Genotype-correlated parental influences in two strains of mice. *Journal of Comparative and Physiological Psychology,* 1963, *56,* 882–886.

Ressler, R. H. Inherited environmental influences on the operant behavior of mice. *Journal of Comparative and Physiological Psychology,* 1966, *61,* 264–267.

Richards, M. P. M. First steps in becoming social. In M. P. M. Richards (Ed.), *The integration of a child into a social world.* London: Cambridge University Press, 1974.

Richards, M. P. M., & Bernal, J. F. An observational study of mother-infant interaction. In N. Blurton Jones (Ed.), *Ethological studies of child behaviour.* London: Cambridge University Press, 1972.

Ringler, N. M., Kennell, J. H., Jarvella, R., Navojosky, B. J., & Klaus, M. H. Mother-to-child speech at two years—Effects of early postnatal contact. *Journal of Pediatrics,* 1974, *86,* 141–144.

Rosenblatt, J. S. The basis of synchrony in the behavioral interaction between the mother and her offspring in the laboratory rat. In B. M. Foss (Ed.), *Determinants of infant behaviour* (Vol. 3). London: Methuin, 1965.

Rosenblatt, J. S. Socio-environmental factors affecting reproduction and offspring infrahuman mammals. In S. A. Richardson & A. F. Guttmacher (Eds.), *Childbearing—Its social and psychological aspects.* Baltimore: Williams & Wilkins, 1967.

Rosenblatt, J. S. Views on the onset and maintenance of maternal behavior in the rat. In L. R. Aronson, E. Tobach, D. S. Lehrman, & J. S. Rosenblatt (Eds.), *Development and evolution of behavior*. San Francisco: Freeman, 1970.

Rosenblatt, J. S. States in the early behavioral development of altricial young of selected species of non-primate mammals. In P. P. G. Bateson & R. A. Hinde (Eds.), *Growing points in ethology*. London: Cambridge University Press, 1976.

Rowan, W. *The riddle of migration*. Baltimore: Williams & Wilkins, 1931.

Rowell, T. E. Hierarchy in the organization of a captive baboon group. *Animal Behaviour*, 1966, *14*, 430–443.

Rowell, T. E. *Social behaviour of monkeys:* Middlesex, England: Penguin Books, 1972.

Ryan, J. IQ—The illusion of objectivity. In K. Richardson & D. Spears (Eds.), *Race and intelligence*. Baltimore: Penguin Books, 1972.

Ryan, J. Interpretation and imitation in early language development. In R. A. Hinde & J. Stevenson-Hinde (Eds.), *Constraints on learning*. New York: Academic Press, 1974.

Salk, L. Mother's heart beat as an imprinting stimulus. *Transactions of the New York Academy of Science*, 1962, *24*, 753–763.

Salk, L. The role of the heart beat in the relations between mother and infant. *Scientific American*, 1973, *228*, 24–29.

Sander, L. W. Regulation and organization in the early infant-caretaker system. In R. J. Robinson (Ed.), *Brain and early behavior*. New York: Academic Press, 1970.

Schneirla, T. C. Levels in the psychological capacities of animals. In R. W. Sellars, V. J. McGill, & M. Farber (Eds.), *Philosophy for the future*. New York: Macmillan, 1949.

Schneirla, T. C. The concept of development in comparative psychology. In D. B. Harris (Ed.), *The concept of development*. Minneapolis: University of Minnesota Press, 1957.

Schneirla, T. C. Psychological comparison of insect and mammal. *Psychologische Beitrage*, 1962, *6*, 509–520.

Schneirla, T. C. Behavioral development and comparative psychology. *Quartelry Review of Biology*, 1966, *41*, 283–302.

Schneirla, T. C., & Rosenblatt, J. S. "Critical periods" in the development of behavior. *Science*, 1963, *139*, 1110–1115.

Schneirla, T. C., Rosenblatt, J. S., & Tobach, E. Maternal behavior in the cat. In H. L. Rheingold (Ed.), *Maternal behavior in mammals*. New York: Wiley, 1963.

Scott, J. P. Critical periods in behavioral development. *Science*, 1962, *138*, 949–958.

Seligman, M. E. P. On the generality of the laws of learning. *Psychological Review*, 1970, *77*, 406–418.

Simpson, G. G. Behavior and evolution. In A. Roe & G. G. Simpson (Eds.), *Behavior and evolution*. New Haven, Conn.: Yale University Press, 1958.

Slater, P. J. B. Describing sequences of behavior. In P. P. G. Bateson & P. H. Klopfer (Eds.), *Perspectives in ethology I*. New York: Plenum, 1973.

Spencer-Booth, Y., & Hinde, R. A. The effects of separating rhesus monkey infants from their mothers for six days. *Journal of Child Psychology and Psychiatry*, 1967, *7*, 179–197.

Sperry, R. W. Mind, brain, and humanist values. In J. R. Platt (Ed.), *New views of the nature of man*. Chicago: University of Chicago Press, 1965.

Spinelli, D. N., & Pribram, K. H. Changes in visual recovery function and unit activity produced by frontal cortex stimulation. *Electroencephalography and Clinical Neurophysiology*, 1967, *22*, 143–149.

Sturtevant, A. H. The behavior of the chromosomes as studied through linkage. *Zeitschrift fur Induktive Abstammungs und Verersbungslehre,* 1915, *13,* 234–287.

Sutherland, J. D. The concepts of imprinting and critical period from a psychoanalytic viewpoint. In B. M. Foss (Ed.), *Determinants of infant behaviour* (Vol. 2). New York: Wiley, 1963.

Svare, B., & Gandelman, R. Stimulus control of aggressive behavior in androgenized female mice. *Behavioral Biology,* 1974, *10,* 447–459.

Tiger, L. *Men in groups.* New York: Vintage, 1969.

Tiger, L., & Fox, R. *The imperial animal.* New York: Holt, Rinehart and Winston, 1971.

Tinbergen, N. *The study of instinct.* Oxford: Clarendon Press, 1951.

Tinbergen, N. Comparative studies of the behavior of gulls (*Laridae*): A progress report. *Behaviour,* 1959, *15,* 1–70.

Tinbergen, N. On aims and methods of ethology. *Zeitschrift für Tierpsychologie,* 1963, *20,* 410–433.

Tinbergen, N. Behavior and natural selection. In J. A. Moore (Ed.), *Ideas in modern biology.* Proceedings of the 16th International Zoological Congress, Washington, D.C., 1965.

Tinbergen, N. On war and peace in animals and man. *Science,* 1968, *160,* 1411–1418.

Tinbergen, N., Broekhuysen, G. J., Feekes, F., Houghton, J. C. W., Kruuk, H., & Szulc, E. Egg shell removal by the black-headed gull, *Larus ridibundus L.,* a behavioral component of camouflage. *Behaviour,* 1962, *19,* 74–117.

Turiel, E. Developmental processes in the child's moral thinking. In P. Mussen, J. Langer, & M. Covington (Eds.), *Trends and issues in developmental psychology.* New York: Holt, Rinehart and Winston, 1969.

Valenstein, E. S., Riss, W., & Young, W. C. Experiential and genetic factors in the organization of sexual behavior in male guinea pigs. *Journal of Comparative and Physiological Psychology,* 1955, *48,* 397–403.

Van der Kloot, W. G., & Williams, C. M. Cocoon construction by the Cecropia silkworm. I. The role of the external environment. *Behaviour,* 1953, *5,* 141–156. (a)

Van der Kloot, W. G., & Williams, C. M. Cocoon construction by the Cecropia silkworm. II. The role of the internal environment. *Behaviour,* 1953, *5,* 157–174. (b)

Vince, M. A. Some environmental effects on the activity and development of the avian embryo. In G. Gottlieb (Ed.), *Behavioral embryology.* New York: Academic Press, 1974.

von Uexkull, J. A stroll through the world of animals and men. In C. H. Schiller (Ed.), *Instinctive behavior.* New York: International Universities Press, 1957.

Vowles, D. M. Neural mechanisms in insect behavior. In W. H. Thorpe & O. L. Zangwill (Eds.), *Current problems in animal behaviour.* London: Cambridge University Press, 1961.

Welker, W. I. Ontogeny of play and exploratory behaviors: A definition of problems and a search for new conceptual solutions. In H. Moltz (Ed.), *The ontogeny of vertebrate behavior.* New York: Academic Press, 1971.

Wiesner, B. F., & Sheard, N. M. *Maternal behaviour in the rat.* Edinburgh: Oliver & Boyd, 1933.

Wilcock, J. Gene action and behavior: An evaluation of major gene pleiotropism. *Psychological Bulletin,* 1969, *72,* 1–29.

Wilson, E. O. *Sociobiology.* Cambridge, Ma.: Harvard University Press, 1975.

Witt, P. N., Reed, C. F., & Peakall, D. B. *A spider's web: Problems in regulatory biology.* New York: Springer-Verlag, 1969.

Author Index

Subject Index

Abnormality, 52
Adaptation, 41
Aggression, 18, 21, 30, 32, 36, 59, 72, 88, 92, 94, 95 (*see also* Fighting)
Analogy, 32, 53, 105
Anatomy and function (*see* Structure–function relationships)
Anecdotalism, 9, 10, 12, 13, 105
Animals as tools, 8
Answers:
  acceptable, 38
  alternative, 39
  appropriate, 38
  criteria for, 38
Anterior pituitary, 19, 21
Anthropocentric orientation, 84
Anthropomorphism, 9, 10, 89
Aphasia, 27
Attachment, 6, 31, 36, 89, 90, 93, 94 (*see also* Mother–infant relationships)
Auditory experience, 102

Behavior, general laws of, 8, 11, 84
Behavioral organization, 19, 45, 56
Behavior genetics, 16, 70
Behaviorist movement, 10, 13
Behaviorists, 42
Biofeedback, 24
Biological basis, 27, 31–33, 35, 36
Biological core, 32
Biological determination, 30, 31
Biological function, 31, 40–42

Biological imperative, 15, 35, 38
Biological inevitability, 35
Biological nature, 29, 37
Biological transducers, 81
Biology and psychology (*see* Interdisciplinary relationships; Psychobiology)
Biometrical analysis, 65
Biopsychology (*see* Psychobiology)

Care of young, 21, 22 (*see also* Maternal behavior; Parental care)
Catastrophe:
  biological, 61
  geological, 61
Causal perspective, 40
Causation, 108
  developmental, 44
  historical, 43
  immediate, 43, 44
  ontogenetic, 44
  phylogenetic, 43
  proximate, 43
  questions about, 41, 43, 87
Circular reactions, 103
Cognitive development, 103
Communication, 44, 90–92
Comparative psychology, 7, 14, 45
Conceptual confusion, 39, 40
Critical periods, 5, 95–97
Cross-disciplinary (*see* Interdisciplinary relationships)
Cross-fostering, 17